MIDLIFE MARGARITAS

Stories from Women Who Made It to the Other Side of 40 and Rocked It

Compiled by Hembree
Shannon Hembree
Jen McGinnis
Bree Luck
Sarah Weitzenkorn
Dionne Williams
Anne Karrick Scott Deetsch
Heather Von St. James
Barbara Fleck
Elizabeth Pendleton
Emily Cooke
Bernadette Jasmine
Vanessa Velez
Laura K. Bedingfield
Beckie Cassidy
Sarah Freeman Knight
Jennifer Porter
Rosanne Nelson
Brooke Schmidt

ISBN: 1542343208
ISBN 13: 9781542343206
Library of Congress Control Number: 2017900090
CreateSpace Independent Publishing Platform
North Charleston, South Carolina

For Heather,
who reminds us that no matter the odds, there is always hope,
and for all the "ordinary" women everywhere who are doing
extraordinary things.

CONTENTS

INTRODUCTION

To our fellow fortysomethings (and all those who will soon be joining our ranks):

You know what they say—forty is the new fifty. No, no, that's not right…they say forty is the new thirty. Which is great, except that most women will tell you that they know a hell of a lot more in their forties than they ever did in their thirties, and despite the wrinkles and sagging body parts, they wouldn't take any of it back. (Do not interrupt with your objections, please!)

In fact, that's why we're here—to hand you a fictional margarita and welcome you to the decade of female knowledge, power, and all-around just-don't-give-a-flying-fig attitudes. You made it here, and you earned every wrinkle, sag, and bag that comes with a life well lived.

Pause for a fictional sip of your fictional margarita, and pat yourself on the back. Now, let's continue.

You are a badass, having made it this far. Life presents a lot of challenges to slog through, and you've made it through forty years of ups and downs. You are the bomb, the shazam, the women of the hour, and we dedicate this book to you.

The following pages convey the stories of real women sharing their journeys and their forty-year-old perspectives on everything from surviving cancer to facing fears to living with depression to embracing the single life. They are the stories of women rising up after unimaginable loss, of overcoming impossible odds, and of finding humor in the everyday challenges women face. They are the stories of women like you, and they are proof that if you dare to dream and laugh and love, life—like wine—gets better with age.

So, cheers to all our sisters out there! This journey is ours to make together. Raise your glass, toast a toast, and let's make it a memorable trip.

Happy forties, and happy reading!

CHAPTER 1

ON RETURNING TO WORK (OR TRYING TO) AFTER RAISING KIDS:
WHITE HOUSE EASTER BUNNY COSTUMES, TONGUE RINGS, AND RÉSUMÉS, OH MY!

By Shannon Hembree

I used to write and edit documents for a president of the United States. I've had freelance clients tell me I am a miracle worker and that I saved their butts. While I have self-doubt in every other area of my life, I feel pretty secure about my abilities as a word-smith. Oh sure, like most people I know who are in this line of work, I have the ongoing internal dialogue of, "Is this good? Oh no, it's terrible…isn't it? But it's kind of good. Or maybe it's crap. Is it good?" But even with all of that, I didn't think getting back into the workforce (beyond freelancing, that is) would be an insanely steep mountain. I didn't think that getting out of the rat race to raise young children would be something frowned upon…a lot.

I was wrong.

I never intended to be a stay-at-home mom. I never sat there in my youth saying, "My aspiration in life is to raise kids." I'm wired for work. I've had bosses actually call me a workhorse. I don't mind burning the midnight oil to get something done right. In fact, I thrive on it.

But then I had a beautiful baby girl. (No, this is not the point where my life plan changed and my brain rewired itself for being a stay-at-home mom.) I had researched day cares for months and found one with a reputation for being the best of the best—the place where you could take comfort in the fact that your child was being loved and getting top-notch care. And they did love my daughter there. Perfect, right?

Nope. My daughter caught cold after cold after cold, and she wound up having to get ear tubes put in when she was nine months old. Inevitably, my husband and I wound up asking ourselves the question that every parent asks at some point (albeit in a variety of different circumstances): "What are we doing?"

And so began our journey as stay-at-home parents. My husband took the first shift, doing contract work from home while he cared for our daughter for a year and a half. When I became pregnant with twins, we knew the time had come to make the swap.

Flash forward five years. My sons entered kindergarten and my daughter third grade. I was...*free!* Sure, I missed my kids during the day, but in more than five years, I hadn't peed alone, hadn't had a phone conversation without little ones throwing tantrums in the background, and hadn't gone to the grocery store without buying a million impulse pieces of grocery-store trash in an attempt to get my kids to be quiet. We never had a nanny or even a regular sitter. It was just me and my three kids. Every day. Every night. Every minute of every day.

Don't get me wrong, I have no regrets about being a mom—not a single one. BUT...I have also scooped vomit out of a sink, paid a babysitter extra when my twin boys took off their poopy diapers and decorated their room, rescued my son from the closet when his twin lured him in and locked the door (in defense of the aggressor in this case, his twin had been pummeling him for weeks), used a bulb syringe to suck snot out of little noses, ridden to the ER in an ambulance with a child who was having trouble breathing, cut crusts off sandwiches, clipped little nails, and done all the things that parents do every day. And while I love that I had the opportunity to do those things, I also looked forward to returning to the "official" workforce beyond the freelance world.

You see, when worker bees lose their work, they're a bit lost. And I had been. I missed being part of a team on work projects. I missed interacting with other adults. I missed conversations that lasted more than five minutes. I missed the work bathroom where small children didn't interrupt with demands that I bring them pudding immediately or offer to flush the toilet for me. Most of all, I missed writing.

Oh sure, I had my on-again/off-again blog with my friend Sarah, but there is something about business writing that I find sexy. Stop laughing. I mean it. I swear, it's fun! And I'm blushing a bit now when I say this—sometimes the geekier and the more poorly written the text, the more fun it is to edit. There…I said it. So, now imagine if you will that for the first time in more than five years, I had before me the opportunity to re-enter that world of work…and to get back to a two-income household where we could actually afford things.

Needless to say, there I was in my breathless anticipation. I dusted off my résumé. I lined up my references. I pulled my best business suit out of its pristine cleaner bag. Truth be told, I pulled it out from the plastic bin it had been hiding in for years, and I made a feverish yet wholly unsuccessful attempt to iron it. I put in an application at a temp agency for writers and editors. And then I waited…but not for long. A woman called me almost immediately to see if I could come in for an interview. Easy peasy, I thought. Clearly, I totally had it in the bag.

But then I got to the interview, and PYT was clearly not happy with my résumé. (The beauty of being in your forties is that you totally get that Michael Jackson reference.) "Why are your writing samples so old?" she wanted to know. "Why are your references so old? Why did you leave your last position?"

Me: "I left because I was pregnant with twins, and then I stayed at home to raise my kids."

PYT: Blank look. Why would anyone make that choice? "Five years off?" her eyes seemed to say. "You're screwed."

The interview was clearly not going as planned.

"I wrote and edited documents for a president of the United States!" I mentally screamed. "Surely that counts for something?" Apparently not so much.

But...back to the interview. PYT's tongue ring was throwing me off, and so was the fact that she couldn't understand why I wouldn't relinquish my current freelance contacts or give her samples of work I had done for them. I tried to explain that I never release clients' documents (I have very strong feelings about a little thing called confidentiality), and I don't use my freelance clients as references. Again, disapproval oozed over the desk between us.

I left the interview with that weird feeling of "What just happened here?" PYT seemed unable to get beyond the fact that my writing samples and references were old. Which begs the question: If that gap in employment is so unforgivable, what are women in their forties (or thirties or fifties) to do if they take a substantial period of time off to raise kids? And equally puzzling to me, why hadn't my husband gotten the same grilling when *he* returned to the mainstream workforce?

In a nutshell, ladies, we are in fact screwed. Or are we? I'm not really sure yet. I'm still on my mission to get back to a "real job," so I'll have to keep you posted on that front. The stories I've heard from other women who've made this journey, however, are less than promising. I'm an optimist by nature, though, so the skies may be a little cloudy right now, but they are not yet dark and gloomy.

Since we all know that you can't make things happen with dreams alone, I'm pursuing my next lead—networking. I can't be sure, but my guess is that if you're a middle-aged stay-at-home mom, having a friend help you get a foot in the door might be more important than it normally would be in a job search. This friend could reassure potential employers that you took time off not because you were in jail (not real jail, anyway, but maybe the kiddie jail where they barricade you in the kitchen with toys while you are trying to figure out a new recipe—not that that's ever happened to me...), but because you really did take time off to raise children.

The other beautiful thing about being a more mature job applicant (and yes, I did laugh while typing that) is that you know shit (yup, laughed there, too). Let's face it—there is something to be said about experience. Case in point—everyone coming out of college will surely know where to put a comma (okay, *some* people coming out of college will surely know where to put a comma), but will they understand the nuances of language? Will they understand that some things that are written perfectly according to the rules of the grammar world are not appropriate to say?

At the White House, we were trained to examine each and every word and phrase for things that were inappropriate or that just sounded off. For example, while "warm greetings to all those..." was a common phrase for starting presidential messages, we never used it in messages to firefighters. Can you guess why? If so, you may be on your path to a career in editing! I also edited corporate documents later in my career where the language was not technically incorrect but—if read in the "right way"—did have an oddly sexual undertone (which, while that can be fun, probably isn't ideal for business-related text). *Penetration*, for example, is a word that should always be used sparingly and with the utmost caution. Just ask the FBI. I have never heard radio personalities filled with as much glee as when they read aloud FBI statements talking about backdoor penetration during the Apple encryption dustup.

The question, then, for potential employers is this: Do you want to entrust your reputation to someone who has no experience in real-world editing, or do you want to go with someone who has an experienced eye? At least, that's the way I am going to spin it.

The other spin doctoring going on inside my head in a repetitive loop (I probably shouldn't mention that in an interview, should I?) is that there is something freeing about being forty that makes me want to take chances in my career that I might not have taken when I was twenty. After all, if it doesn't work out, what are people going to do—laugh? I have worn maternity underwear. If ever there was a moment when you learned to laugh at yourself, it was then. My inspiration for this is my dear, sweet Sara Blakely, the founder of Spanx. (See how I made that connection there… with the underwear and the underwear lady?) I saw an interview in which she stated that in her view, failure was about not trying, not about the outcome. And I like that. At forty, we're old enough to know that there are people out there who are going to laugh at us. And hopefully we're old enough at forty to smile right back when they do.

But seriously, who cares if you fail? Okay, of course we all do, but Sara Blakely is right—we should care more about *not* trying than we do about trying and failing. We should be comfortable enough in our own stretched-out, baby-ruined, age-damaged skin at this point in our lives to throw caution to the wind and say, "Fuck it, I'm going for it!" (But only in your head, because a lot of people don't like it when you drop the F-bomb.) And seriously, why not go for it? At forty, we're likely halfway to the grave anyway. So, who's with me (on the saying fuck it part, not the grave part)?

And I *have* thrown caution to the wind. While I was home with my kids, I wrote a young-adult novel that I am pitching to various agents. So far it's been mostly crickets in response (fingers crossed on the initial nibbles!), but I am out there trying it. My husband actually figured out the odds of my getting an agent based on the figures one agent put out there, and I think it's safe to say that my odds of getting published in the young-adult market at present are pretty daunting. In fact, I probably have a better shot at being a Victoria's Secret model at this point. On the bright side, I have never in my life wanted to be a Victoria's Secret model (although no doubt my husband has a different take on this). Despite all that, I'm glad I wrote that darned book. I'm glad I threw caution to the wind and did it, even if it winds up being only for me. Because sometimes those are the best kinds of crazy adventures. Unless I do eventually get that book published—then *that* will be the best kind of crazy adventure. Just like this book, which was also a half-baked loaf of crazy before we jumped off the ledge and did it. Just like every woman in her forties needs to jump off the ledge (not literally!) and do something crazy in her career path of choice at least once.

In keeping with my forties theme of throwing caution to the wind, I am also toying with the idea of expanding my freelance work by making cold calls or sending marketing letters to local associations and corporations. What is the worst thing they can do—say no thank you? Not reply? Ahem…sounds a lot like what I have gotten from a lot of agents on the novel front. And do you know what happened when I got rejected there? I survived. Not only that, but when they offered suggestions for improving my novel, they were right. Just like Sara Blakely is right. Failure isn't the outcome; it's the not trying.

Who wants to look back and wonder why they didn't take that career path they always wanted but were too scared to try? Not me. And really, the embarrassing and the tried-and-failed moments make the best stories. For example, it's all well and good to say that I worked at the White House, but do you want to know the two stories that are the real crowd pleasers? I'll give you a hint—they have nothing to do with the documents that made my soul sing. Oh no, not those. They were these two little gems. First, the president's dog—yes, dog—peed on the floor of my office. Yes, peed. Second, being a total dork, I really wanted to dress up as one of the Easter Bunnies at the White House Easter Egg Roll. I don't know why. Maybe it's because of my love of little chocolate bunnies. Maybe it's because my inner dork doesn't know where to draw the line. Whatever it was, I wanted to do it.

So, there I was in the West Wing, dressed in my bunny finery. I was getting instructions for going on stage, and I was hanging on every word, not wanting to screw up my one chance at bunny glory. And then someone more important showed up. Before I could say hippity-hop, I was helped out of the bunny costume so that Molly McImportant Person could dress up like a bunny and go get all of the glory for herself. Don't worry, I'm not bitter...not really... because I recognize that those really embarrassing stories are what make life interesting. They make us human, and they teach us how to laugh at ourselves. And that is just the kind of attitude you need when you close the door on your stay-at-home-mom job and put yourself out there again on the employment front.

We fortysomething-year-old women also need to remember that a lot more is possible than we sometimes think. (Do men have this same problem?) Sometimes we limit ourselves—and let others limit us—by embracing a false set of expectations, and once we slap the "impossible" label on a situation, we give up before we even give whatever it is a try. If, however, we pull on our brave, big-girl panties (more like our *big* forty-year-old-woman panties) and push the line for what we think is possible, we may find ourselves dabbling in the impossible.

When I was a staff assistant at the White House, one of my bosses (yes, I was that low on the totem pole that I had a veritable roundtable of bosses) told me I should apply for an editor position after I kept finding mistakes in documents. My very insecure self laughed (very nervously) at that, and I told my boss all the reasons why I was not a good fit. When I finally gave in to her incessant nudging and went to pick up the editing test, my other boss (they were everywhere!) told me flat out that I wasn't what they were looking for but that I could take the test if I wanted to. She told me in no uncertain terms that they wanted a "professional" editor with "formal editing training." Needless to say, I was not...and I had none. But, for whatever reason, my editing test impressed them—which is funny, because on paper, I was in no way qualified for the job. It was a job I was never supposed to get. I took the leap anyway, and in doing so, I found a hidden talent that I have been reveling in ever since that day.

I could come up with some clever line here, something about if you just believe in yourself, all your dreams will come true—but we all know that's crap. (Too honest?) Because really, you don't have to believe in yourself—not 100 percent, anyway—in order to achieve the impossible. Sometimes what's required isn't a complete lack of self-doubt (because who has that, anyway?). What's required is closing your eyes, taking a deep breath, and shouting, "Screw the odds! I've conquered periods, maternity underwear, and nursing bras!" (But not around men, because that shit makes them uncomfortable) and then jumping in and going for it, come what may.

So, go ahead and jump on in. Write the book you've been putting off writing, even if it winds up being just for you; reassess your career path if you feel like you're stuck in a rut; recognize that while you may not be in a place to spend every waking hour in the office to advance your career, you have experience that can make you an invaluable asset (in that, I just saved you from saying sexually suggestive things in your corporate-newsletter kind of way); and above all, remember to laugh. At yourself. At life. At kid poop on the walls. At everything that comes your way. Because if laughter really is the best medicine, you need all of that shit you can get.

You're halfway to the grave, after all. And we're right there with you! *Slainte!*

✦

Shannon Hembree used to be a stay-at-home, freelancing mom of three. Many months after writing this chapter, she got a job offer from some lovely women at a nonprofit organization. She is not at all bitter about never having been a White House Easter Bunny, and now that she's fortysomething, she embraces the idea of living fearlessly...unless the situation involves heights, spiders, snakes, public speaking, or anything else that crosses the boundary for sane living.

CHAPTER 2

ON LOVE AND LOSS AND LOVING AGAIN:
REDISCOVERING JOY AFTER THE LOVE OF MY LIFE DIED

By Jen McGinnis

At some point every day, I remind myself how lucky I really am. Anytime something small and irritating happens, I do a little brain blink to remind myself that I have a life I never saw coming. I have a wonderful, funny, accepting, loving husband and a fabulous, inquisitive, sensitive, loving son. We live on a tropical island in the middle of the Pacific Ocean, in a great place on the water with our very own dock. I consider myself extremely fortunate in innumerable ways. But my happiness was hard fought and not without heartbreak.

I was married once before, pregnant with another child once before—and I lost both of them in the same year. My miscarriage that fateful February was disheartening, disappointing...so many things, but really it was just plain-old sad. I felt fortunate, though, because when you tell girlfriends about a miscarriage, you find out that many of them have had a similar experience or at least know someone who has. Most of my friends also had healthy children, so at the time, I felt my then-husband, Alex, and I had plenty of time to try again.

It was not to be.

It all started with pain. Back pain, leg pain, night sweats, doctors' appointments, x-rays, and physical therapy, plus a visit with a specialist. All this came to a head on a night out on a boat with friends for the annual BayFest celebration at Kaneohe Marine Corp Base in Hawaii. After a great night at a concert with friends, drinking and boating, Alex and I waved good night and stopped off at the restrooms before I was going to drive us home. He came out looking a little upset. His pants were soaked, as if he had lost control of his bladder. I was alarmed and, being the designated driver, insisted on going to the ER.

Alex was angry, and I had no idea which way the hospital was, so we argued back and forth until he agreed to give me the directions and go to the ER. We sat for hours. I think they had actually forgotten about us, which did nothing for his mood. Finally, they took him in for an interview and testing. He underwent an MRI, and we waited there for the results. I thought they would come back out and say it was just a disc bulge, but instead, a neurologist came in and told us they were seeing something at the very top of the MRI and wanted to do another one. We waited some more, and then the neurologist returned and said, "I'm sorry, but there is a tumor of some sort in your spinal canal."

Everything is a little fuzzy after that. I remember both of us crying and saying, "What are we going to do?"

The doctor admitted Alex so that he could order the testing immediately. I called his parents, and everyone was nervous and upset. After being admitted, Alex had some of the tests, and the doctor recommended a biopsy to determine the type of tumor. Our next step was to decide if we would go off island for treatment, but Alex didn't want to uproot and go for testing at another facility unless we had to. There was also some concern over flying and pressure from the tumor.

Alex said, "No matter what we do, if it turns out badly, we'll wish we had done something different. I want to stay here unless we have to go."

For the record, he was right. I have often wondered if I should have pushed harder to go somewhere else. Done something different. Been more insistent. Many, many things, really.

But we stayed. We cancelled a previously planned trip to another island for our friend's wedding, and Alex's surgery was scheduled. We talked about my getting him new shoes. He kept walking out of his slippers because he couldn't feel his feet. It made us smile, because he would just drop a slipper with a step, which was funny to see—but it also made my heart ache, because I knew it meant the tumor was putting pressure on his spinal cord and decreasing the feeling in his legs. On the Fourth of July, we walked around the hospital and watched the fireworks display from a balcony. They were gorgeous. He stood behind me with his arms around my shoulders and neck, and I cried silent tears.

His mother flew in for the surgery and, after a harrowing trip, made it while he was still in pre-op. We talked together for a while, and then they injected some medications to relax Alex before surgery. As they wheeled him to the operating room, his mother kissed him. When I bent down to do the same, he looked into my eyes, staring intently at my face and trying to say something. There I was, a complete emotional wreck, thinking he was going to express some deep and meaningful words of love. So, I leaned in closely to hear the words he was forming. "You have two mouths," he said with utter fascination and seriousness in his voice. Not the words I was expecting, needless to say.

"Then I'll give you two kisses," I said, and then I did.

When they'd wheeled him into surgery, I turned to my mother-in-law and burst into tears—the uncontrollable kind of tears that come from trying to hold oneself together for too long.

After the surgery, the pressure on Alex's spinal cord increased. He had a second surgery, and then loss of feeling and then loss of the ability to move. He was transferred to a rehabilitation center with the anticipation of months, even years, until recovery.

While at the rehabilitation center, there was a spinal-fluid leak, and Alex returned to the ICU. There was another surgery and then an infection, which was followed by another surgery.

Alex's mother flew home with plans to return with his dad. Siblings had begun plans to visit one at a time to keep his spirits up for the long haul. One of his brothers and his family had already visited. It was forty days of worry, stress, and fear.

My mother was also on moral-support duty and flew in to help. One night, after my mom had left Alex and me alone for the night in his hospital room, he had a seizure.

Oh, my God, what just happened? He was gone and then back in less than ten seconds, and I was yelling at him, "Are you all right?" He had no idea why I was so upset. I started barraging him with questions. "Do you know where you are? Do you know *who* you are? Are you all right?"

Before he could finish answering, there was another event—an eyes-rolling-back-in-his-head, mouth-making-a-noise-a-child-makes-when-pretending-to-be-a-large-truck, and spit-coming-out-of-his-mouth kind of event.

At that point, I had already yelled for the nurses, who were completely confused as well.

"Are you going to call a code?" I asked.

They weren't sure of the protocol in such a case, since his heart was still beating even though he was incoherent. I was completely unhinging, yet I was able to answer all the code team's questions. Type of surgery, dates, allergies…

And then Alex was awake and alert again. They checked all sorts of things and then intubated him. His final words were "Malignant hypothermia runs in my family!"

This statement is actually irrelevant to his story, but it breaks my heart because his last concern was a worry about this condition that had afflicted a family member after exposure to general anesthesia. He was frightened. Did he realize in his last lucid moments that something was very wrong?

He said this just before they intubated him, before the pulmonary embolism, the cardiac arrest, and the seemingly never-ending chest pounding that occurred during the hour-long resuscitation effort. It was before the temporary relief at his brief recovery of heart rhythm and his transfer down to the ICU, where they started the whole process again. Did he know in that moment that something was very wrong? Was he really afraid?

After the transfer to the ICU and the ongoing efforts to stabilize him again, I remember the doctor coming out and telling me what was going on. As a physical therapist, I understood more than enough of what they were saying to each other to be terrified and horrified—and also to be aware of how badly things were going at that moment.

They don't put bicarbonate of anything into someone's bloodstream unless things are going badly. They did that to Alex twice to try to balance the acid levels in his blood, because there was too much carbon dioxide.

The doctor was explaining the situation. Unable to…something. Carbon dioxide levels in his blood…something. No blood to his brain…something. Not able to maintain a heartbeat without medication…something.

"Are you asking me to call it?" I said to her.

She looked genuinely shocked and said, "No, I would never do that. I'm just letting you know things do not look good."

Now when I think of it, I hear myself as though I am in a terrible made-for-TV drama. Why had I said that? I think I was just so utterly confused. My brain could not process all that it had just seen. How could this be happening? We had accepted that life would change, that there would be challenges to recovery, that we would need to adapt. Hell, I am a PT. I already had a rehabilitation plan all figured out. I had it all figured out right up until the doctor came out a second time and told me there was nothing more they could do. That she was sorry.

I watched the code team leave looking tired, dejected, angry, frustrated—feeling all the feelings the actors on TV try to portray.

When everyone was gone, I went to Alex's bedside and laid my head on his chest. It felt normal. It actually felt like a relief. I hadn't been able to lie that way for so long, ever since his surgeries, which had left him sore. I had missed it.

I begged him not to go at first. Then, when they turned off the ventilator, I told him not to worry. "Don't be afraid," I cried. Then a minister came in.

"I don't think I'm going to want to talk to you!" I practically yelled at him. He was young, maybe thirty. Younger than I was, I think. He looked genuinely upset and just asked softly if I'd like him to say a prayer. "Oh, that would be nice," I told him.

The doctor returned and asked if I wanted him to remove the intubation tube. "Yes," I said, but I didn't watch. Alex looked so normal then, relaxed even. At peace? Maybe. God, I hope so.

I lay there with him until death slowly crept over his body, and it began to feel bad to stay. He didn't look like himself anymore. *What do I do?* I wondered. I didn't want to just leave him there all alone. I was unable to move.

My mother and uncle took me to my uncle's place, and after a stiff whiskey, I broke my in-laws hearts and spread the suffering along to all the other people who loved him.

We planned a funeral in Hawaii, another at his work's Los Angeles office, and still another in his hometown. Everyone came.

Everyone was sad. Everyone really did love him. I never realized how much you have to share a person when they die.

It also turns out that dying is a complicated process. Credit-card companies will close accounts if you are only the secondary account holder. Banks will freeze your assets if you don't transfer all the money to another account before they find out. Your mortgage needs to be changed. Everyone needs a death certificate. Some people will continue to send mail and bills no matter what you do, but some student loans get forgiven. How nice.

I spent the next year close to madness. I drank and smoked cigarettes and didn't wear a seat belt. My extra bit of rebellion—like daring death to go ahead and come for me.

I talked to a friend one day and told her that while I could be trusted not to harm myself, I would embrace something terrible happening to me. I imagined contracting a terrible illness and being relieved at not having to continue waking up every morning feeling as though I had been stabbed through the heart.

When I was at work one day, a colleague commented on how wonderful it was that I even wanted to be at work. Given that I had in fact paid the first month's mortgage on a home I no longer needed (and certainly couldn't afford) from the hospital room after Alex's first surgery, I told her nicely that I didn't *want* to be there but that I *needed* to work.

"What do you want to be doing?" she very gently and sincerely asked.

"I want to run around in circles screaming, but eventually I would get tired of running and screaming and come to a stop, and I would still be in the same place. So instead, I come here and work."

"Oh," she said and started typing.

Time went on. Friends and family called and visited and coordinated. Some flew across the globe to spend long weekends with me. They listened to me on the phone and checked in when I hadn't called in a while. They sent me cards. One sent a funny card because there was too much sadness already, and she knew I would get that she gets it and that it would be another special moment.

I remember making the choice to see beauty in beautiful things. I saw people that I didn't want myself to become—mean, angry, resentful people who missed all the beauty around them because they were blinded by their grief. I read a gazillion self-help and grief-management books. I sought solace in my in-laws and our mutual grief and disbelief that the world could in actuality be so completely unfair and indiscriminate. They were beyond generous and loving toward me.

I avoided seeing a counselor, which in retrospect was a mistake, but slowly I regained myself. I realized quickly that I had become a different person. The woman I used to be had died that night alongside the man I'd loved. My sister came out to visit a year later and stayed for nine months. We had a really great time, although we spent too many late nights hanging out in hammocks on the back porch, drinking and lamenting.

Then she got her dream job and moved to DC. I was left in a big house with a bigger mortgage, so I decided to rent out half the house. I got two tenants. Then I decided I wanted to think about a family. I hadn't met anyone. In fact, I hadn't even gone out on a date, but I had made the decision that I wasn't going to sit and wait for my life to pass by and regret not even trying to enjoy things while I had the chance. I was going to have a baby. And not a "hey, I think I'll have a baby to try to fix things" baby. I wasn't sure about finding a man I could love again, but I knew I could love a child, and if the right guy eventually came along, he wouldn't mind if I had a child, anyway.

I told my uncle about my baby plan. He thought it was a great idea and promised lots of baby stuff for the future fabulous child.

Two days later, he called me up and asked if I was sitting down. The conversation went something like this:

"Why, what did you do?" I asked him.

"I know a guy that I think you should go on a date with."

"Okay, so where did this guy come from, and why are you suddenly thinking this is a great idea?"

"Well, I met him playing golf."

"What? Like yesterday? You get one chance to set me up on a blind date. Are you sure you want to use it up on a guy you just met the other day playing golf?"

"It was a really long game of golf."

What the heck, I figured. At least after this, I wouldn't have to tolerate his setting me up anymore. So, my uncle sent me this guy's information, a couple of pictures, and what was essentially an informal CV.

The mystery guy in question had a lot of things going for him. He was good looking, educated, and—according to his work history—motivated and successful. We exchanged e-mails for a while, and unbeknownst to me, my uncle threatened him that he had to be careful with me.

We ended up e-mailing and talking on the phone over the next three months. I was traveling. He was traveling. He had company. I had company. We finally settled on a lunch date over the Labor Day weekend. I will throw into this story that he was in fact ten minutes late to this date, but once we sat down and ordered, we had a really nice time. He asked me out again for the next night. Dinner this time. Hmm...

The next night, we had a great time at what has now become a regular favorite dinner spot for us. A fantastic slack-key guitar player entertained us as we ate our meal and sampled some local microbrews. My date asked me to go to dinner again during the week to a downtown brewpub where there would be more live music. I agreed happily, but now I began to panic. When and what should I tell him about Alex?

Date night arrived, and I was so worried about how to share my story that I could barely eat. I finally just gave him the condensed horrible story about Alex and ended by telling him, "That's it. That's my story. I can't do anything to change it. I loved my first husband, and he was a good person. But I have decided that I don't want to waste my life, and I don't want to spend the rest of my life alone."

He listened intently and then looked at me and said, "That sounds like a good idea," and casually took a bite of his dinner. Just like that. No negativity, no judgment, no jealousy.

I remain amazed to this day at his unflinching acceptance of my reality. Later on in our relationship, I went through the blow-by-blow account of what had happened, and Craig looked at me with genuine love and sadness, remarking on how horrible that had to be for me. My man is really wonderful.

After a whirlwind romance and just under a certain someone's one-year dating requirement, we got engaged on an amazing trip to California and then got married nine months later with wonderful friends and family on a gorgeous beach in Hawaii. We celebrated the night under the stars, dancing our final dance to a Rascal Flatts song with the lyrics, "God blessed the broken road that led me straight to you," which basically sums up how I feel. And yes, I cried.

Fast-forward four years, and here I sit at my computer on a lazy Sunday morning, writing this chapter and sipping my morning coffee as my beautiful son drags my wonderful husband out onto our lanai to search for pirate ships coming our way. I am blessed beyond measure. Life continues to smile on me. I couldn't have imagined that I would be here today, but I am madly in love and so glad to be right where I am, even though the road here was arduous.

So if ever you find yourself at what seems like rock bottom, take heart! Turning forty is no big deal, and you never know what is around the corner. Life can be difficult and even cruel, but if you remind yourself to look, you will see that beauty is all around you, even in your darkest moments. And love can find you, even more than once, if you allow yourself the risk—and decide to wait ten extra minutes for lunch.

⇥⊹⊹⇤

Jen McGinnis is a physical therapist and co-owner of an outpatient physical-therapy office. She is married to a great guy, and they have a fun, fabulous little boy. They live on a tropical island in the middle of the Pacific Ocean and wake up most days to sunshine and warm breezes.

CHAPTER 3

ON TAKING THE PATH LESS TRAVELED:
HOW I JOINED THE CIRCUS, WENT TO PRISON, AND ARM WRESTLED MY WAY TO A JOYFUL LIFE

By Bree Luck

It was just before Thanksgiving, and my husband, Geoff, and I were driving down the Georgia coastline to visit my family for the holiday. I was in a foul mood. In my late thirties, I was still a struggling actress and had been working with a new talent agent. She had scheduled several great commercial auditions in the preceding weeks, but I hadn't booked a single acting job. I feared I was losing my mojo. Even more, I wondered if I'd ever had any mojo to begin with. Our children were sleeping in the backseat, and Geoff was trying to help me out of my funk.

"How come I still don't know what I want to be when I grow up? I'm too old for this," I whined. "Something's wrong with me."

"You're an actor," he reminded me. "You don't have control over these things. You do the best you can, and then you just wait."

"I don't want to have to *wait* to be extraordinary."

He nodded. We had been through this before. Audition weeks typically provoked emotional maelstroms—but lately there had been fewer periods of reprieve.

"I don't think I want to be an actor anymore," I blurted out.

"So quit acting."

"But I don't know how to do anything else."

"Okay, then learn. You're smart. You're capable. What's holding you back?"

I pouted, sullen as a teenager. I wasn't supposed to feel this way. I was a mom. I was going to be forty soon. I was supposed to have had my act together by now. Instead, I felt like a failure.

"Start from scratch," he said, ever the optimist. "What are your dreams? We used to dream together all the time. Let's do it again. If you could do anything..." He trailed off encouragingly.

I stared out the window, watching the sun crest over the marshland.

"I don't know if I even have any dreams anymore. It's that bad."

Most kids want to be an actor at one point or another. It's like being a basketball star or an astronaut—only I'd never grown out of it. I had been a lonely bookworm of a child, and the greatest moments of my young life occurred in the dusty but joyful Little Theater of Gastonia in North Carolina, where I sang, danced, and played my way into some semblance of a social life. I wanted to prolong that fantasy life on the stage, where I felt connected to the people around me, valued by the cast, and loved by the audience.

There was one significant problem with this plan that no one pointed out to me: I was not a particularly good actor.

I'm still not sure why no one ever told me this hard truth, but it is probably because they thought I would grow out of this silly dream and do something practical once I got to college. My parents tried to talk me out of it. My mother insisted I would get bored with theater, and my dad mentioned something about it being such a difficult industry to crack. I wasn't worried about getting bored, though. Nothing was more exciting than the thrill of a performance. As for breaking into the industry, I knew it would take only one big gig to find instant success. I ignored the advice of my parents and approached my young-adult life with the very naive but powerful American worldview that if I worked hard enough, anything was possible.

At age nineteen, I committed myself to doing all the things you are supposed to do to live a fantastic, extraordinary, movie-star life. I took classes (well, I took one class). I pored over audition notices and diligently sent my headshot and résumé along with a witty-yet-sincere cover letter to everyone who had an address. I dyed my hair blond, bleached my teeth, and worked out every day. I practiced foreign accents on strangers in airports, and I belted out entire musicals in the car. I moved to New York, got myself a couple of temp jobs for flexibility, and then, armed with obnoxious earnestness...I waited.

One of the unfortunate aspects of being an actor is that you are generally always waiting. Waiting for someone to discover you. Waiting for auditions. Waiting for phone calls. Waiting to book a job. Waiting to perform. Waiting for a review. Let me tell you, waiting wears down a soul. Years of waiting tore away at my self-esteem. I was living with constant anxiety and the sense that I could never, *ever* do enough, that the reason I wasn't successful was because of an unfortunate combination of being basically unlucky and fundamentally unworthy. While my self-esteem was regularly beaten down by this worldview, I gave birth to two kids and trudged into my late thirties.

Now, riding down to Georgia for Thanksgiving, I found myself bemoaning every career choice I had ever made. I was tired of waiting for my life to begin.

What is it about our culture that propels us toward expecting the extraordinary? We strive to be our best selves, to fit in, to have our houses and our cars and our closets in order—but we also demand to be special, to stand out, to think outside the box. We belong to the generation that saw movie stars become world leaders. We were raised by superhero women who juggled seemingly impossible tasks of running corporations *and* taking care of their families. We were the girls who tried to starve ourselves to model perfection while still being strong enough to kick a soccer ball around the field *and* maintain a clear head for killing the SATs. Even then, even if you did everything right, there was no proof that your efforts would be enough. *You* didn't determine how extraordinary you were—you had to wait for the world's validation. How did we come to have such unrealistic requirements for ourselves? What would have happened if we had simply released ourselves from those expectations and allowed ourselves to be normal? Was it giving up to accept that I was ordinary?

Not long after this trip, a dear friend invited me to see a show in town—a circus, actually. Like many people, I've never really enjoyed circuses. I'm not into the animal-training thing, and clowns freak me out as much as anyone, but this circus was different (no animals, no clowns). Really, it was a freak show / art installation / interactive theatrical extravaganza with fire dancing, stilt walkers, and raucous music set in an old, crumbling warehouse. Watching it was a transformative experience.

Here were people breaking all the rules of theater that I knew. In this crumbling space, found objects became works of art. Faux-bearded ladies approached audience members, bestowing kisses on anyone who was willing. A band called Accordion Death Squad filled the air with Ukrainian folk melodies set to a bluegrass rhythm. If I'd ever doubted the power of a work of art to change a life, here was proof that it could. As fire dancers playfully spun their balls of flame into the air, I felt something in my soul give way. It was a visceral experience, akin to falling in love. The world was brighter, sounds were more complex, and I was looking at the world through fresher eyes. These bold artists weren't waiting for the audience's approval. They were creating—and enjoying—their own extraordinary moments.

As I drove home from the circus, I knew what I needed to do. The next morning, I identified four core desires that would make my normal life feel extraordinary, and these I wrote in bold lettering on a sticky note by my computer:

Every day, I want

- *creative connections,*
- *a little bit of danger,*
- *control, and*
- *to help people.*

I made up my mind to stop going to commercial auditions. I called my agent and told her I was taking time off. For the next few weeks, I focused instead on trying to fulfill each of these four desires every day. I found that I was already committing to small actions that satisfied these needs. Something as minuscule as giving directions to a tourist fulfilled the desire to help people. Trying a new workout class at the gym felt a little bit dangerous. I took the practice deeper. Instead of walking along a sidewalk like a normal adult, I played balance beam on the curb along with my kids. My husband and I had impromptu dance parties in our kitchen while we cleaned up after a dinner party.

Once I started exercising this muscle of attentiveness, the world was brimming with opportunities to meet desires—and my need for living an extraordinary life was gradually supplanted by the thrill of fulfilling core desires in everyday actions. I had let go of struggling through life as an actor—and instead relished the freedom in taking action. Although the routines of our days had not changed very much, our home became more joyful.

Buoyed by the spirit of the renegade circus and the success of these small changes, I took the plan one step further and e-mailed one of the organizers of that wacky troupe, arranging a meeting in a local coffeehouse. Jen, the circus mastermind, sported a neon-pink bob and exuded "cool" the same way I exuded "mom." Over our chai lattes, I convinced this powerhouse of a woman to let me do something—anything—for her troupe's next event. Since I didn't breathe fire or walk on stilts or fly the trapeze (yet), there wasn't room for me as a performer, but having been an actor for almost twenty years had left me with a wealth of production experience. I was pretty good at keeping my diaper bag organized, and I was fearless about striking up conversations with just about anyone, so Jen asked me to produce the damn thing.

We spent the next nine months in various living rooms, coffeehouses, and warehouses putting together a second circus. I learned that I was a pretty good producer. I was adept at communicating with stagehands and designers and performers and musicians and freaks and property owners and investors. I could coerce Hula-Hoopers who lived in tents and smoked weed for breakfast to make it to rehearsals on time, but I could just as handily convince the fire marshal that despite the abundance of pyrotechnics in our act, we were absolutely not going to burn down the building. It was hard, grueling, nonstop work, but how satisfying it was to be the one in control!

To be clear, it had never, *ever* been my intention to actually produce a circus, but by taking on this pipe-dream project, I found that many of the desires I had craved from acting—connection and creation and a little bit of danger—were being met professionally as well as personally. I had taken a small but significant leap and landed feetfirst in the middle of joy.

⇒≒╪≒⇐

Producing Shentai helped me take control of my creative life and reinforced my confidence to step into the unknown. Once it came to an end, though, it was time for a new project. Although I loved the circus life, I still felt the driving need to help people—to effect change. When a theater company in our town sponsored a drama group in a maximum-security women's prison, I reflected that this project had the potential to meet all my core desires (control, creativity, danger, *and* helping people), and I seized the opportunity to make theater with inmates. Soon I was behind bars as the lead teacher and creative director of a program called the Voice Project, where inmates wrote, rehearsed, and performed original (as well as established) poems, plays, and songs.

Our group started small—the first session had only five women in it—but in time, it filled to capacity, and inmates approached me in the halls, asking when the next session would begin. We created a waiting list for the program, and when we held performances, nearly every inmate in the prison attended. Some of the effects of the Voice Project were quantifiable—violent and nonviolent infraction rates among the group members dropped dramatically. Some results were immeasurable. Women serving life terms for murder quaked in fear before a performance and danced with glee when the audience cheered with delight over a moving poem or a particularly humorous moment. After each session, women would testify that the Voice Project had changed their lives.

The inmates were growing from this experience, and so was I. Once, a week before a performance of *Macbeth*, we had a "shakedown" in our class. Two officers interrupted our dress rehearsal to search every pocket, every pant leg, every shoe, and every cap of each woman in the project. I watched as these dedicated participants were so insensitively handled by the officers. When the search had produced a pack of crackers, two bags of M&Ms, and a love letter, five key members of the group were written up for infractions and suspended from the program for six months. As she was being searched, one of the women looked over at me and whispered, "It will be okay." But it wasn't okay to lose all that we had worked for over such petty possessions. I was devastated.

We had lost nearly half our cast members with only a week to spare before showtime. The day after the siege, I met with our small, sad group and asked the inmates what they needed in order to feel a sense of completion after such a big blow to our production, telling them there was no shame in quitting. But these intrepid women refused to give up.

In truth, I had been ready to cancel the show. It would be impossible for us to proceed with the original script, and we didn't have the time to rework an entire play. But the women were determined to create a new play that honored their work. With hearty resolve, they pulled out all the materials that we had used in our preparations: character sketches, imaginary letters from the actors to the roles they were playing, translations of Shakespeare's monologues into raps, prop lists, scene notes, diary entries—and together we took these materials as well as the original text and created a new script that told not only the story of Macbeth but also the story of our little drama group. As these eight remarkable women performed the downfall of the Scottish lord in front of two thousand inmates, they also told the story of their own fortitude and success. Through their choice, these prisoners taught me about the beauty that can be found in failure and the importance of honoring all that is good.

Six months later, the inmate who had whispered to me in the midst of being searched returned to the group, and I asked her why she had risked getting into more trouble by reaching out to me in that moment. We stood in the hallway before the class started, watching another inmate waxing the linoleum floor in wide, wet circles.

"You just looked so sad. So hurt. And I knew I had those crackers and that I was gonna get busted…stupid me, carrying stupid crackers. I knew better than that. And I just wanted to let you know that I was sorry. Sorry for messing it up. I've done a lot of shit in my life, and I'm really trying to turn it around. But sometimes you push the rules a little bit, and you get busted—and someone gets hurt. And all you can do in that moment is say you're sorry."

When I'm feeling beaten down by failures, I remember the strength of those women—the ones who were caught with crackers and candy as well as the ones who'd thrived despite the setbacks. With those inmates in mind, I try to remember to apologize for my mistakes and make the most of what I have. Because only then can we feel free.

I'd been working in the prison for a couple of years when I got a call from pink-haired Jen from the circus, who approached me with a new proposition. She wanted to start a ladies' arm-wrestling competition, which she called CLAW (Charlottesville Lady Arm Wrestlers). Her basic premise was this: Once a month, a bunch of local women would dress up as strong and funny female personae and arm wrestle at a local diner. Audience members would buy CLAWbucks and place their "bets" on the wrestler they wanted to win. At the end of the match, all the money collected would be donated to a charity. The wrestling would be real, but there were plenty of opportunities for antics. Cheating was encouraged. Would I do it?

I had never even won a thumb-wrestling competition, much less an arm-wrestling one. But I was trying desperately to raise money for the Voice Project. Instead of waiting for more funding, here was a chance to take action. So, I made a deal with my persuasive friend: I would wrestle if the Voice Project could be the recipient of the first match's proceeds. She agreed.

I could have chosen any character, really, but I needed to call upon my inner badass, so I developed a sort of dominatrix, superhero, spy—a cross between the girl in the Kill Bill movies and Catwoman. I hired a trainer and ordered hair extensions, a catsuit, and a pair of six-inch stiletto heels from WickedTemptations. com. In the bathroom of our little house one cold evening, I transformed into Stiletto Southpaw, a character who would command respect.

Sixteen-year-old Francis was babysitting my children the night of the first match. She babysat for us frequently and was used to seeing me in my typical uniform of blue jeans and a blouse. This night, I sat on the side of the tub in the bathroom, worrying about how to get past the babysitter while looking like a prostitute.

I thought back to my core desires.

What did I really want in this moment? Clear communication. Respect...and to get to the wrestling match without Frances calling social services and having my children removed.

"Hey, Frances?" I called to her through the door.

"Yes, Mrs. Luck?"

"Um...I just want you to know that no matter what I look like tonight, I'm still just a normal mom, okay? I'm telling you this because when I was a teenager and I was babysitting, if a mom came out looking like I'm looking right now, I'd be very, *very* concerned."

"Um...okay?"

"And there's no need to post anything about this on Facebook or anything, okay?"

"Okay."

"And I will tip you very well tonight."

"OKAY!"

When I pushed open the door, having transformed from do-gooder mom to a six-foot-two vinyl-clad vixen, Frances's eyes may have widened considerably—but her mouth stayed shut.

⚊⫷⫸⚊

I had not expected a large crowd at the Blue Moon diner that night, but when I arrived, the place was inexplicably teeming with people. My adrenaline surged. Up against Sidewinder, the snake lady, I lost in the first round, but the night was a success. The proceeds from the match covered the entire yearly operating budget of the prison project. I signed up to wrestle the following month, and the next, and the next, and even though my rotator cuff screamed with pain after a particularly gruesome standoff with Bridezilla, I fell in love with the strength I felt when I was arm wrestling.

My arm grew stronger, and CLAW grew larger. Soon we were raising thousands of dollars for women's initiative projects every month. As the matches grew in popularity, I began to internalize the most important lesson I could learn from being a dominatrix superhero arm wrestler: even if your ass gets kicked, pose like a winner.

CLAW received national attention, and we started popping up in newspapers and magazines around the country. A national organization was founded, and new arm-wrestling groups arose in Chicago, Los Angeles, New Orleans, and Washington, DC. A documentary about lady arm wrestlers toured the festival circuit. This scrappy little idea had become a national phenomenon as women all over the United States unleashed their hidden superhero personae to raise money for charity. After a couple of years, I hung up my stilettos, but not before *Penthouse* magazine decided to write an article about this charity sensation.

⚊⫷⫸⚊

Not too long after I "retired" from charity arm wrestling, I got a phone call from my mother.

"I got the goods," she said in her best spy voice—but I knew exactly what she was talking about from the glee in her voice.

I pulled the car over into the Best Buy parking lot. This was a moment I wanted to savor.

"Wrapped in brown paper?" I asked.

"White, actually. I had Charlie pick them up from Barnes and Noble. I thought I'd get some strange looks if I went."

"I'll bet."

"Would you be too embarrassed if I posted it on the refrigerator? It's not every day that your daughter appears on the pages of *Penthouse* magazine."

Just hearing my mother say the name of the magazine made me blush.

"It's not me that's mentioned, you know. It's my alias."

"Darling, you're all over the Internet. Everyone with Google will know that Stiletto is you."

"Everyone who actually reads the article in *Penthouse*. Do people really read the articles?" I didn't wait for an answer. "There are no pictures, right?"

"No pictures. Just a story about you and your arm-wrestling friends. Very well written, I might add."

I smiled into the phone.

"So, I can put it on the refrigerator?" she asked. "I'm just so proud."

If I've learned anything, it's that you can't go through life waiting for the approval of others. You can't wait for your life to suddenly become extraordinary, but you can take small steps to take control of your desires. You can learn great lessons from unexpected people. You can learn to look and feel like a winner even when you fail. I've also learned that when you take a path that is uniquely yours and someone you love wants to celebrate that, there's no harm in sharing the joy.

"Go ahead," I told my mom. "Heck, you can even frame it."

━┼┼━

Bree Luck is a mother, theater director, and amateur arm wrestler. She is always looking near and far for the next big adventure.

CHAPTER 4

ON BECOMING A CAREGIVER FOR A PARENT:
BEING THANKFUL FOR WHAT IS LEFT, NOT LAMENTING WHAT IS LOST

By Sarah Weitzenkorn

As kids, we come to expect that our parents will be there for us. That's how it's supposed to work. Young or old, we're supposed to be able to call them up for advice, for a laugh, or for a shoulder to cry on, because no matter how old we get, they're still our parents. Only it doesn't always work that way. Sometimes it's the kids who do the caregiving, who shoulder the burden for life-altering decisions, and who take on the parenting role for their own parents. That's how it went for me, anyway.

I guess I always knew Alzheimer's would come calling in my family again. But knowing something will happen and having it *actually* happen are two totally different things.

It was right before Christmas in 2009. With divorced parents—my husband's parents were also divorced—we alternated our Christmas visits with our moms, since our dads had both remarried. That Christmas, it was my mom's turn to make the six-hour drive from North Carolina to Georgia. Since we had two toddlers, we had reached the point where our families were coming to us, which I was more than happy about.

The night before my mom was supposed to drive to our house, I called her to confirm what time she was leaving. The conversation was fine until she asked me what road to take.

"The one to Charlotte, Mom," I replied. "Forty-nine."

"Where is that?"

Those words stopped me cold. My heart started racing. My palms got sweaty.

My mom had grown up in North Carolina and had lived in her town for more than three decades. Now she didn't know how to get to the highway she had been on a million times before.

After a restless night, my husband made the six-hour drive up to North Carolina. He picked up my bewildered mom and drove her all the way back to our house.

And so it began.

I remember what happened over the next few months through a bit of a haze—and it's not from the wine I consumed many nights. There were appointments with doctors, tears, phone calls, more tears, worry, confusion, and anger.

A few short months after that fateful Christmas, my sixty-nine-year-old mom was diagnosed with Alzheimer's disease. I knew it was coming because her mother had had it. She had died from complications associated with it about fifteen years prior. As her mom suffered through it, my mom had taken care of her.

And now it was my turn. At thirty-eight years old, I became the caretaker.

Our relationship had always had its fill of ups and downs. My mom had raised my brother and me largely by herself, and now that I'm a mom, I realize that she was stronger than I ever knew. We clashed growing up, and I never really felt that she liked me.

Loved me, yes—but I wondered many times if I was someone she liked to be around. I went off to boarding school at a young age and drove myself to college. She wasn't one to make a big fuss about my getting married or driving down to help me pick out flowers or a dress for the big day. She just told me the night before I got married that she hoped I hadn't chosen a strapless dress, because it wasn't classy. I had to laugh as I walked down the aisle in a beautiful ivory strapless gown.

As an adult, I spent many years working through that. I had a great therapist who taught me to deal with my issues—and the fact I loved Little Debbie Oatmeal Creme Pies way too much—so I was at a pretty good place when my mom was diagnosed with Alzheimer's disease. My mom and I had finally reached the point in our relationship where we were friends. I would call her for advice and visit her often. We were in a good place.

After my mom's diagnosis, my type A personality served me well. I took over her checking account, got the house put in my name, contacted a real estate agent, and researched where we would go from there. I did all of this with two small children and a part-time job from home. And wine. Did I mention wine?

None of this was easy. The wine was helpful, but so were friends and attorneys. During that Christmas trip when I knew what was coming, we got a power of attorney for my mom. In my heart, I knew that I would have to make critical decisions for her down the road, and that power of attorney is now a worn-out piece of paper. I have used it more times than I can count over the last several years to manage everything from her credit cards, bank accounts, and insurance to her retirement fund and social security. Companies would not even talk to me unless I had it, and thankfully I did. I also had a friend who was an estate planner who helped me navigate getting my mom's house and other assets put in my name. I tapped into the expertise of my wonderful friends and asked for advice from people who had been on this road. I also read as much as I could about elder care and educated myself on anything I thought might be useful.

But all this "expertise" was only helpful to a point when it came down to the more emotional part of it. I knew, for example, that taking away my mom's car keys would be one of the harder parts of this process. My mom has always been a very independent woman. She cleaned out her own gutters, power washed her own house, and now, at barely seventy years old, it was my job to take away what she relied on the most: her car. I went with her to the Department of Motor Vehicles to help her renew her license, and when my mom wasn't looking, I snuck up to the desk to talk to the supervisor and let her know that instead of a standard renewal, my mom needed to take the driver's test. She failed. While her heart sank, mine literally broke. I then took the next step, which was taking her car away from her, and her dependence on me grew.

Early on in this process, a good friend of mine told me that the best lesson my young children could learn from this was that we take care of the people we love. My children don't understand Alzheimer's. Hell, *I* don't understand Alzheimer's, but I am always reinforcing to them that even though their grandmother's brain doesn't work like everyone else's, we still love her, and we will always take care of her and make sure she is okay. In the many restless nights that followed that troublesome phone call with my mom all those years ago, it is that bit of wisdom from my friend that gives me comfort—that out of this, my children will learn the value of care and compassion. And that is no small blessing.

Not long after my mom's diagnosis, we sold her house and most of her furniture. We moved her into an apartment a mile away from us and started a new and vastly different adventure, with me in charge of my mom's diminished life. I am not sure if there is a way to describe what it's like to take care of someone who is slowly forgetting everything, but I will say that it takes a lot more patience than I brought to this chapter of my life.

Although I was not one to ask for help, I quickly realized that I had to, and thankfully, those who loved me were more than willing to jump in. I juggled taking care of my mom and taking care of my young children with the help of wonderful friends and a supportive husband. It wasn't comfortable for me to ask for a helping hand, but it was necessary.

My mom only lasted a year in the apartment we'd found for her nearby. A few too many times, the stove was left on, and we decided it was time to find a place where she could be supervised more closely. The next step was an assisted-living facility about an hour from me. She seemed to do well at first, but after about a year, she began trying to flush her underwear down the toilet, and the staff suggested it was time for the next phase— memory care.

The first few years after her diagnosis, my mom still knew who I was when I went to see her—so much so that she'd always remind me that I looked *much* better with lipstick on and not so gently suggested I try hers. As the years went on, her slipping memory started to include her memory of me, and I found myself begging for a reminder from her of how much better it would be if I had a good pale pink for my lips.

You see, one of the hardest things about Alzheimer's disease is watching the person before you lose her (or his) memory. Conversations with my mom have always been the hardest part for me. As she progresses, she asks me many times who my mother is. I gently tell her who she is, and although she acts excited, she is also puzzled. She tells me how her parents picked out her outfit for the day even though her parents have been dead for many years. She has no idea what year it is or what state she lives in. She can no longer watch television because she can't follow along. Even so, I find myself telling my mom, with pride, about my children's latest milestones or a funny story about what they had recently done. In that split second, I am speaking to her as if she is really "all there" and can understand. It's a hard habit to break, but just as soon as I finish telling her my story, she gives me a blank stare that is a harsh reminder of the depths of her disease. It makes me miss her so much—even though she is right there.

There came a point in the midst of it all when I finally decided I couldn't juggle the many things on my plate, even with help. The long days with my mom and the kids, the long nights in front of a computer for work, the lack of exercise, and the abundance of bad food caught up with me. When you are a mom, you sacrifice yourself for your children. When you are a mom *and* a caregiver of some kind, you sacrifice even more. I finally let go of my job that I loved so much, joined an Alzheimer's support group, and resumed the therapy I'd given up all those years ago. As we moved into the next stage of my mom's care, I finally felt that I was getting control back, and that control included care for myself. It's vital. Without taking care of myself, I don't think I would have survived this as long as I have.

I also learned that doing things for others helps, and I give back when I can. I raise money for the Alzheimer's Association and help other young mothers caring for family members through various blogs and websites I am involved in. Helping others navigate this journey gives me some sense of purpose and makes me feel like my experience with Alzheimer's has value.

Now, as we enter the last phase of my mom's life and her disease continues to progress, I try to hold on to the laughter and the humor that my mom can bring. She has no filter, and she will let the waitress know that her hair is a mess or will tell me how much she needs a man. She has trouble getting words out most of the time, but many times when she makes herself laugh, she has a smile that can light up a room. She laughs with me a lot, and although she refers to me as "a nice girl that comes to see her," seeing her joy when I visit each week still makes me happy. The woman I once felt wasn't happy with me is filled with delight when I walk into the room. It is amazing how life can come full circle in so many ways.

Even with these moments of brilliant smiles and joy, my journey is not an easy one. I am a fortysomething-year-old (no need to get specific here) daughter who is shouldering the burden of caring for a parent with Alzheimer's disease, and while there are days when it consumes my every waking moment, I am so much more than that. I am a mom who is teaching her children the value of caring for those who can no longer care for themselves. I am a friend who understands that sometimes you are in a position of having to ask for help, and sometimes you are the one in the position to help. I am a wife who is living the phrase "in good times and bad" with a husband who is amazing enough to embrace those times with me. I am a resource for others in the same dreaded Alzheimer's boat. And I am a woman who is learning the value of caring for herself while caring for others.

Watching my mother slip away is heart-wrenching. Anyone who has been a caregiver for a parent knows that. I could get lost in thoughts of how far into the depths of this disease my mom has fallen. But instead, I am choosing to savor the good days. I am treasuring the little moments and the shared laughter. Rather than lamenting what is lost, I am thankful for what is left.

Sarah Weitzenkorn is a stay-at-home mom of two children. In addition to liking piña coladas and getting caught in the rain, she loves girls' weekends, mindless celebrity gossip, and oatmeal creme pies.

CHAPTER 5

ON ROCKIN' THE SINGLE LIFE:
WHY SIPPING LEMONADE ON THE BEACH IS ALWAYS BETTER THAN PLUNGING LEMONS OUT OF THE TOILET

By Dionne Williams

I was engaged once...

I was in my midthirties, and he was a really nice guy. I can't take that away from him. He was sweet and caring, but I learned certain things about him—and about us, and about me—while in that relationship that brought the engagement to an end. One thing I learned was that having your own self-esteem isn't the only thing that's important; the person you're in a relationship with must have self-esteem as well. And he didn't. He seemed to feel that he needed to continually get his friends to like him (even though they already did), so he sometimes went "over the top" as a friend. For example, he wanted to give $2,000 as a wedding gift when a friend of his got married. I told him I thought that was a bit much for a gift. He said he thought I was being a little selfish. That conversation turned into an argument, and I ended it by telling him to ask his brother's opinion. Needless to say, his brother agreed with me.

The conversation about his going overboard wasn't a new one for us. We'd had conversations before about his paying a bar tab for others and paying for dinner at a restaurant when other people were clearly pulling out their cards and telling him not to. It was at this point that I knew I was dealing with a man with a self-esteem issue, someone who didn't just want but *needed* acceptance from other people. A few therapy sessions and some long talks later, I found myself back in the single lane and starting over. I traded in that chance for the fancy white wedding dress and the stereotypical fairy tale that society thinks every woman wants in life for a chance at *real* happiness—the happiness found in not settling for someone you *know* will drive you crazy in the long run.

I learned a lot of things about myself on this journey. (I like to call them adventures, because relationships can be like that.) The first thing I learned is that making a list of what you want in a man and what you want in a relationship really helps. After making a list, pray on it, look at the list again, and then cut it down to the top five items. Then comes the next—and most important—part: stick to your list!

The E-Mail Adventure

About two months after the engagement meltdown, I started hanging out with a few men, just trying to enjoy myself. (A girl can't just sit at home during the summertime!) I started spending more time with one guy in particular—he made me laugh, and he and I had good conversations. A bit about him: he was a little older, a member of a fraternity and another service organization, and a full-time graduate-school student.

At that point, I had not made a list of what I needed in a man or relationship. I was just going with the flow. So, Rob (names have been changed to protect everyone's chances of one day making it onto *The Bachelor*) and I were dating, but time and his oddly low standards of cleanliness were an issue. Now, I know a single man may not have the cleanest house, but most people know that you must clean the bathroom or else there will be…yuck. Just yuck.

Yuck #1: The bathroom that most of your guests use—the one in the hallway—well, his looked like it had barely been cleaned… ever. Maybe not even in the last century. Dirt had piled up in the sink and in the toilet (enough to leave a ring). Take a minute and think about that—how much time must have passed for an actual *ring* to have built up in that sink and in that toilet? Worse yet, what were those rings made of? My mother came over at one point, and her "Oh, goodness!" said it all.

Yuck #2: When you have carpeting, you have to vacuum so that dust and dirt don't build up. Judging by the state of his floor, no vacuum had been introduced to it in years. Hmm…let's just say I wore socks or my flip-flops the entire time I was there.

Yuck #3: Another pet peeve of mine is a dirty shower. I mean, how long does it take to clean your shower? A little Comet, a sponge, a little warm water, and *boom*—it's clean! His wasn't, and every time I took a shower at his place, I wore my flip-flops.

Yuck #4: If the pipes in your house shake and shudder when you flush the toilet and a slight smell of mildew is evident, you might have an issue that needs to be addressed—a big, stinky, shaking, and shuddering issue.

Looking back, that I allowed myself to deal with all that for so long amazes me. That was my mistake—and a lesson learned. I should have known right then that it was time to run for the hills.

Another mistake I made was not recognizing that we just weren't on the same page. He was always occupied with studying and attending functions, and there never seemed to be a break. Sometimes almost two weeks at a time would go by before I saw him again, and I seemed to take a backseat to his studying, his fraternity stuff, and his other service organization. Now, don't think I didn't understand. I went to graduate school and worked a full-time job—and I had even dated a guy who had a daughter, whom I helped out with sometimes. And by "helped out," I mean that I got up early to take her to school and then went to work, studied, came home, cooked dinner, and went back to studying. I did all this *and* had papers due every week. But the guy in question didn't seem to be able to do it—or maybe he didn't want to do it. Either way, it seemed there was always a paper due or a function going on—or that he was going out of town for a convention. There was time for everything but me.

It took months for me to decide that I'd finally had enough. In the midst of a conversation one night, I asked, "What do you want to do as far as a relationship? We've been seeing each other for some time, so the question I want to ask you is, do you want to be with me?"

Sounds simple, right? I guess not. After that conversation, I didn't hear back from him for over a week, and when I did, it was in the dead of night.

On a Tuesday morning at 2:00 a.m., my phone buzzed, waking me up. I turned over and took a look and found an e-mail from Rob. It said, "Because of school and my commitment to the other organization, I think I will not be able to give you the relationship you want. I'll be doing a lot of traveling and will not have a lot of time. I'm sorry I am doing it this way, in an e-mail, but I felt it would be less drama. I care about you a lot."

At first, I was shocked. Then my shock turned to anger—not about what he'd said, but about how he'd said it. Why the hell couldn't he talk to me like a man? I had to talk to someone about it, so at 2:15 a.m., I called the only person I knew who might be up: my West Coast sister Bonita. When she answered the phone, I proceeded to give her the details about the guy and read her the e-mail. And then, as we always do with men, we laughed and joked about the situation. Men I can live without, but I need my friends.

I didn't call Rob back, but I did reply to his e-mail, saying, "When we last spoke and I asked you to think about the relationship, I wasn't expecting an e-mail. I thought we were adults, and we should be able to talk like we are grown-ups, not hide behind an e-mail."

I never got a response, but I did have a run-in with him two weeks later at his house when I went there to pick something up for my mom. He gave me a hug and said, "You are mad."

"No, I'm not," I responded, and he repeated it again. I simply told him, "No, I'm disappointed. Since I came to you as an adult, I was looking for the same thing back—a little respect—especially since I didn't come at you being nasty. But that's not how you wanted to respond. So, no worries." And that was where I left him.

The Loss-of-the-Man-Card Adventure
Three months later, I got a friend request on Facebook from a guy named Ken, who was a friend of a friend. He was kind of cute, so I took a chance and accepted his request. We went back and forth in an online conversation, and then he gave me his number to call him. We set a first date for the next night, and that first date led to a two-and-a-half-year relationship. (And you thought all the action was on Match.com!)

Many parts of the relationship were good. We did have our moments, though, and sometimes, when certain things occurred, I just had to scratch my head. For example, how do adults not know how to properly plunge a toilet? Don't just sit there and look at the water until it starts to overflow—plunge man, plunge! He also had no idea how to use a drill or that when you come back from the gym, you have to hang up your wet clothes so the funk won't set in. I should have taken away his Home Depot man card at that point.

I laugh at some of these things because my dad was in the military, and he taught me how to properly clean a bathroom (tub and sink), clean a kitchen ("Make sure you run your hand over the counter," he would say), and how to use a power drill along with all the other tools in the toolbox. There were a few things my father could not do, and one of them was washing clothes. I remember one time he washed our clothes while my mother was away on a work trip, and he ended up shrinking one of my favorite pairs of pants and putting something red in with the other clothes, which all ended up pink. My mother came back and took him off laundry duty, telling him never to touch the clothes again. So, over time, as I found out little things about men here and there, I couldn't help but laugh.

But back to Ken…when Ken and I finally decided to move in together, we had to clean out his apartment. He was a big procrastinator and always waited until the last minute. He didn't start packing until the week before the move, telling me, "Oh, it's really not a lot of stuff." He wouldn't admit it, but he was a total pack rat. Boxes and trash bags were everywhere in his apartment. I was trying to be helpful with the packing, but it was ridiculous, and we still had to deal with getting the U-Haul, packing it up, and moving his things into the house. It was an interesting day.

During the time Ken and I lived together, he never cooked in our kitchen. He ate out for breakfast, lunch, and dinner almost every night. I cooked dinner at least three times a week, but he would always pick up food on his way home after the gym—the reason why, he told me, was because it depended on what he felt like eating after his workout. At one point, I told him he was spending too much money eating out every night. However, it was something he had been doing for quite a long time, so I let it be. I cooked for myself and had food left over for the next day, which was great. "You don't have to eat my food, you crazy man!" I would say to myself. Only now, looking back, do I see that maybe *I* was the crazy one for putting up with someone so different from me for so long. I have to say this—I do think that sometimes common sense passes by us when it comes to relationships. It's there one morning but gone the next.

I remember one day coming home and using the downstairs bathroom. When I flushed the toilet, I saw that the water was backing up. (You may have noticed that toilet problems seem to go hand in hand with my man problems.) I got the plunger and started plunging the toilet. It was then that I noticed pieces of lemon coming up. What the hell? I mean, lemon juice maybe, but actual chunks of lemon? I stopped what I was doing, picked up my phone, and called Ken.

"Did you put pieces of lemon down the downstairs toilet?" I asked.

And, as if nothing were wrong, he replied, "Yes, I always do that."

I think I actually looked at the phone when he said that. All I could think was, "Am I seriously hearing this right now?" But nope, big fat nope—I didn't get mad. I put on my sweet voice and told him, "No, babe, you do *not* put lemons down the toilet. They will clog the pipes, which has now happened."

I don't know if there was much more to say after that. I was angry but laughing at the same time. It was too much.

Lemons aside, things might have gotten better in the relationship had communication between us improved or had he even seen that there was an issue. Neither happened.

And then there was an emergency with his mom. She had collapsed in her apartment in New York and had to be rushed to the hospital. Ken drove to New York to see what was going on, and when he talked to the doctor, he found out that his mother had not been taking care of herself. She had stage-three ovarian cancer along with other health issues that she had let go. It was as if she had just stopped living. Because of her age and other issues, the doctors could not put her through surgery. On top of it all, Ken and I were supposed to leave for Europe the following month for my parents' fiftieth wedding anniversary. Everything was paid for and set to go. I didn't ask him any questions, letting him decide what he wanted to do.

We did go on the trip, and while we were away, his mom got worse. We got back on a Sunday, Ken visited his mother on

Wednesday, and she passed on Friday. We buried her a week later in her hometown in South Carolina.

The next few months passed slowly, and we fell into a routine. I knew he was hurting, but he didn't talk to me. He didn't really talk to anyone. Even though I was trying to be supportive, he would tell me, "You don't know what I'm going through, so you can't understand."

This disconnect around communication happened on many levels. Before we'd moved in together, we'd had a discussion about marriage and kids, and at that time, both of us seemed to be on the same page. But after his mom passed, we would go back and forth on the subject of marriage and kids. It seemed that his mind-set about what he wanted had changed. At that point, I was just looking for a yes-or-no answer from him, but he seemed not to understand that. I even arranged for us to go to a relationship counselor to help with our communication. I wanted to make sure that we were talking about things and hearing each other, because I didn't think he was hearing me.

We went back and forth like that for many months. Along the way, other things happened within the relationship that fueled my anger. For instance, he didn't know how to balance his relationship with me and his relationship with his daughter; to him, it seemed easier to keep the relationships separate, which really wasn't working. He left me out, which should have been a clear signal to me at the time that I couldn't make lemonade out of those lemons. Finally, I decided I'd had enough and ended it between us.

After the breakup, I took a few months to myself and then jumped back into dating. It's been more than two years since then—more than two years that I haven't been in a relationship. Some people will tell you this is a sad place for a woman in her forties to be. Society has its own outdated clichés about always being a bridesmaid and never a bride. Everything around us tells us that to be single is to be unhappy. And I could be if I chose to. We could all be unhappy—married or not—if we chose to. But when it comes down to the reality of being in a bad relationship versus being in no relationship, I'll take no relationship every time.

And yes, dating is a mixed bag. It's frustrating as well as interesting. Some dates were truly not worth my time. There have been some weird guys you wouldn't want to be out with after dark, and there have been others who were smart but had no common sense. So, the journey continues.

When it comes to the crazy world of dating, I will say it again: "Make your list, pray on it, cut it down to the important things, and stick with it." This will help you keep your sanity and avoid some of the crap dating involves. Being single in your forties isn't always easy, but it is freeing. And when you're feeling down, keep this in mind: it's always better to be drinking lemonade on the beach in Miami—or wherever else your single self has the freedom to travel—than plunging lemons out of the toilet.

Dionne Williams is a nonprofit project manager extraordinaire. Her co-workers tell her she has the biggest, brightest smile in the office, which could be because she tries to stay positive and lives life one day at a time. In this crazy world, she simply laughs a little, lives a little, and embraces whatever adventure comes her way. It's all about the journey.

ASK THE AUTHORS
WHAT MISCONCEPTION ABOUT TURNING FORTY WOULD YOU LIKE TO DISPEL?

Shannon Hembree

That after you turn forty, you become invisible. (Someone I know once said this to me.) I don't think that is true at all. You are as relevant as you want to be—maybe not in the same ways you once were, but in other ways—ways that I would argue are much more meaningful.

Jen McGinnis

I think a really big misconception is that all the fun will be over and that it's time to be serious. I do go to bed earlier, but I also laugh more easily and appreciate just being with people I love—both friends and family. Life is a gift, every day. Being forty means you are lucky, because there is only one alternative to getting older.

Bree Luck

That forty is the new thirty. What the heck? We earned those years—don't take them away from us! The beauty of having more years to call upon is that we can take a longer view on life, simply because we've seen more of it. Annoying moments, frustrating people, and leaner months all have less of an impact when we can view them as nothing more than weather patterns over these many years.

Sarah Weitzenkorn

That you are *old*. For so long, I thought that turning forty meant getting your AARP card. It's not. You are wiser, stronger, and better than at any other age.

Dionne Williams

I think one big misconception is that if you haven't gotten married or had children by the time you're forty, it will never happen. I don't think that is true. I see many friends getting into relationships and having children either near forty or after forty. Just because it didn't happen yet doesn't mean it won't. I still date and hang out with my friends. I love *love*, so I won't be giving up just yet!

Anne Karrick Scott Deetsch

That you are stale at forty. That you've hit the age of no change. When you decide to get rid of all the baggage and open your eyes with the brilliance of experience, you can find magic in the clarity and humor of age.

Heather Von St. James

That forty is when you finally "have it all together," or that you are over the hill at forty.

Barbara Fleck

That your best years are behind you. These *are* your best years! You are a fully formed woman—physically, mentally, and emotionally. And you still have the vivacity to use that power to make a mark on your world.

Elizabeth Pendleton

That I would be an adult and have it all figured out. Wait…what? Well, I am an adult, but I'm busting my butt to keep trying to figure things out. Who knew there would be so much?

Emily Cooke

I used to think that women in their forties were winding down. You know—middle-aged, slow, boring. But that is a big, fat lie. Forty is *not* old. There are some wrinkles, but I was worried I would *feel* old, and I don't feel old. In fact, I sometimes forget that I am in my forties and think I am still in my late twenties or early thirties. Old is a state of mind—not always a number.

Bernadette Jasmine

I think the biggest misconception about being forty is that it is the beginning of the end. For me, it was the beginning of the beginning. Turning forty provided a second chance at life. Things had already hit rock bottom, so there was nowhere to go but up! Turning forty is not the start of the winding down of your life; it's the start of the fine-tuning of your life. You begin to discover what makes you happy and what you are passionate about—and you stop sweating the small stuff.

Vanessa Velez

That you are old! Forty is a number. Yes, gravity doesn't cooperate anymore, and those extra pounds are a little harder to get rid of, but I feel stronger, more confident, daring, wiser, and in control. I can't fight it, so I am embracing it—and looking forward to what fifty will throw at me!

Laura K. Bedingfield

Remember all the hype and fear about Y2K? Fueled by Prince's anthem to the start of a new millennium, we were all convinced that it was about to be party over, oops, out of time. I think women view turning forty with the same sense of impending doom. We all woke up on January 1, 2000, to our same selves in our same world, doing the same things we'd always done. While turning forty is certainly a milestone, it's not a tombstone.

Beckie Cassidy

That forty is the beginning of the end. I actually feel like I'm finally an adult, like I'm just beginning my adulthood. And with that comes the freedom to do what I want with my (limited) spare time and not feel guilty about it.

Sarah Freeman Knight

Turning forty is actually not a big deal. You still look like you're in your thirties, and nothing really changes. Turning forty-five is horrifying, though! As my daughter recently pointed out, "Mommy, when you round up, you are fifty!" But I'll leave that for another book.

Jennifer Porter

It's difficult to pick one misconception, since they are all equally oppressive and debilitating. However, the worst of the worst is that hitting forty signals "the end of all the good stuff" when the fact is that it's really the beginning of your next forty years. The second runner-up is that you should have it all figured out by the time you turn forty. Stern reminder: drop "should"; its use generally leads to harm.

Rosanne Nelson

This is not your mother's forty!

Brooke Schmidt

I think it's a misconception that you'll suddenly feel grown up at forty. While I am more confident because of my experiences in life, sometimes I still wonder how I'm qualified to have a house, pets, or kids!

CHAPTER 6

ON DEPRESSION AT FORTY:
FINDING SOLUTIONS WHEN YOU CAN'T WISH IT AWAY OR WAIT IT AWAY

By Anne Karrick Scott Deetsch

B aby feet are so beautiful. As are tiny hands and bellies. And is there a better smell than sweet baby skin? As the mother of four children, I have loved each of my gorgeous babies, and like all mothers, have delighted in their very essence. Motherhood is so full of love and wonder. For me, however, it was also full of deep sadness due to the postpartum depression I experienced after the birth of my third child—a sweetheart of a boy and a wonderfully creative and funny child. I thank God every day for him and his brothers and sister, but when he was around six weeks old, the usual feelings of delight turned into anxiety and ultimately a terrifying case of postpartum depression.

The crushing anxiety I felt during the day while taking care of my newborn and his two brothers was overwhelming, and I didn't know what to do or why I felt this way. I loved my baby, but I began to have thoughts that he was not as cute as the other two at this age. He was fussier than they had been, and I couldn't put him down. I felt my loving, mothering self being consumed by this un-named feeling that boggled my mind. How had I—lover of babies and seasoned mother—gotten here? And where was *here?* I loved my husband and children so much. Why was I so miserable?

I should explain that depression runs in my family. My sister has it, and so did one of my grandmothers, who was hospitalized for a year of my mother's life. It was never discussed except in hushed conversations and mild we-are-not-sure-what-she-had terms. Can you imagine being hospitalized for something for a full year and not being able to discuss it? I can't. Growing up in my immediate family, we discussed everything. I do this now with my own tribe, which can be especially trying for my slightly reticent fourteen-year-old son.

As I look back, I can see that this condition manifested itself differently in my younger sister and me. In my sister, depression looked like what one might expect. She slept a lot, cried a lot, and was generally unhappy during depressed periods. For her, depression manifested itself when she was a teenager. Counseling was sought, and ultimately medication was provided. Both continue to be needed and helpful. She is a delightful person, and if you met her, you would never know—just like you would never know if a friend or acquaintance had it unless they chose to share it with you. That is the nature of the beast in us; its presence is there but hidden due to the associated stigma, the perception that the person with depression is somehow weak. And there's no denying this perception is out there. If it weren't, we wouldn't hear phrases like, "Why doesn't she just get over it?" as if depression were something people could just shake off if they set their minds to it.

Weakness is something no one ever wants to exhibit. To be a weak person is to be one of low character and one who is pitiable. This was the prevailing notion in my family at times. It was not stated in so many terms, but it was subtly understood. Strength was always praised. In this atmosphere, it seemed shameful to be less than the pillar of strength that was held up as the example of how to be. I gave myself the hardest time, because I felt I never measured up. Today this feeling is nearly universal in teenagers—albeit in a more temporary realm—but the issue with true depression is that it never goes away, because the perspective that comes with age does not allay those fears.

My depression likely started when I was a teenager, but as one therapist put it, I was quite adept at masking it. It could have been the usual pain and angst of those adolescent years, but my experience says otherwise. Thank God my school insisted on students participating in sports regardless of ability. Exercise is a wonderful, natural way to fight depression and has always worked well for me, albeit temporarily.

Another depressive episode occurred when my beloved father died. Dad and I were very close. He gave me such love, understanding, and faith—faith in God and in myself. I will forever thank him for the gift of faith, as it is such a part of who I am. My connection to my dad continues through our shared faith. When I am in mass, I feel more in touch with him. As I grow older, it becomes more essential. Losing him suddenly from a massive heart attack was the worst thing that has ever happened to me. A part of my soul died with him, and it was devastating. I was completely bereft. My family and I grieved his loss and tried to make sense of it all. Our faith pulled us through the tragedy.

At the time, I was married and had one son. I felt like I was functioning underwater, in a fog, unable to breathe, and many other sad but true clichés. Since my son was still just a baby, his schedule suited my life in that moment—rise, feed him, off to work/childcare, home, feed him, go to bed. It was simple enough to keep him entertained, but my husband had a zombie for a wife. I knew that something had to change.

After several months of feeling such loss and sadness, I sought out a counselor. In all honesty, she was not much help. It's hard to find a good therapist or one who is good for you. Time marched on, however, and while I'm not sure that time heals all wounds, it does lessen the pain. The pain in my stomach from my father's loss is still there. I've just learned to live with it. I implemented the tools I had at hand: talking, prayer, and food. I gained weight. It was eat, pray, love: the depression edition.

I know that what I experienced is very common for people who lose loved ones. Depression from loss is, of course, normal, and what I had was not different from others. My sister felt similarly, but she was at home with our mother, having transferred colleges. I think this helped her—to be at home, sit in my dad's home office, and process it with our community. Living in another state, I felt adrift. Members of my extended family who lived close to me tended toward the strong, silent side of things. For example, when we gathered for dinner on the anniversary of my dad's death, he was not even discussed.

My grandparents took his loss very hard and were unable to speak of it much. I think it must be generational, this belief that it is better to be strong and not express the loss and sadness. My grandmother felt that talking about him—how fun he was or the things he'd said—was too hard. Expressing the grief was too hard. None of us wanted to upset her or my grandfather more than they already were, so we didn't talk about my dad. My grandmother is a strong person in her own way, and I appreciate how she has negotiated through life, but I also know that holding things in is not how I operate. I like to think that when we get together, which is often, she is free to feel those feelings and work through the grief. Now, at least she is able to talk about it and tells me that I remind her of my dad—how fun he was and how easy it was to talk to him. I take this as a great compliment.

My most troubling time dealing with depression definitely came in the form of postpartum depression. I noticed that something was wrong in the weeks after my third son's birth. When my oldest was born, I had gone through a difficult labor and delivery. I saw my son right after his Caesarean birth, but then he was whisked away for a bath, and I went to recovery. It was all a blur—I had been awake for well over twenty-four hours and needed to sleep in order to function at all. I woke up, and when my husband showed me our little bundle, I wept for joy at this tiny boy who was surely the most beautiful baby in the world. Although I felt this same feeling for my later children, I realized there was a distinct difference in that I did not continue in my delight with my third baby. His birth had been a scheduled C-section, and all went swimmingly. Nursing him went well after the usual start-up pains. I can't do a lot of things, but I think I could nurse an army of babies. The problem was that only in my arms would he calm down, and I needed those arms for his older brothers. I wound up putting him in a Baby Bjorn, and we were fine…except not really.

I found myself on an increasingly short fuse with my six-year-old, who was the best little boy. He was loving, sweet-natured, and fun, and his mom was becoming a crazy person in front of him.

One night I remember holding the baby and crying about some silly thing that my six-year-old son had done. In the middle of this upset, I looked from my husband to my son, and they both had the same expression of sadness and bewilderment. I was so upset with my son, and I will never forget the look on his face. He was so little—they all were so little. My middle fellow was in the midst of it, too—just three years old. The guilt from this moment remains with me even now.

In that moment, I realized that the constant anxiety I was experiencing was abnormal. Being their mother was so important to me, and on good days, I reveled in it. This episode demonstrated that I was having mostly frustrating and sad days. The feeling that everything was hard was for two reasons: life with three boys aged six and under *is* hard, particularly when one is an infant, and it was even harder because my brain chemicals were completely out of whack. To me, my sweet baby was not so wonderful. Of course I loved him, cared for him, nursed him, sang to him, and held him for hours on end, but that only made me feel like I was becoming an attachment parent—a method of parenting that was problematic because it coincided with a case of unrelenting postpartum depression. The result was a weepy mom who had a short fuse and couldn't make any decisions.

In the midst of all of this was a rapidly approaching monthly dinner with some lovely college friends. As was our custom, we rotated picking the restaurant, and it was my turn. My town is full of delicious places to eat, so this is anything but a difficult task. Even so, I can remember calling my husband in tears after dropping the kids off at school because I couldn't pick a place to go. This was a particularly low point for me because of the mundane nature of the task. It was a simple dinner for my girlfriends, but I was acting as if it were for world leaders and that I would be kicked off the island if I made the wrong choice.

That's how depression works—it takes normal, easy thoughts and makes them a jumbled mess with completely unreal consequences. Small things become insurmountable, and large things are just ignored and shoved into a deep recess of the mind. Negative thoughts go into a loop, seeming to never end. It is difficult for me to write about this, because even as I write it, I'm thinking, This was not that big a deal. What is wrong with you for thinking this way? And then, of course, my anxiety rises.

Once I accepted that official help was needed, I sought it. This turmoil had to end. Thinking back on the marvelous time I'd had with my other sons, I knew something was wrong and that life with these boys could be so much better. I took the first step, only to hear a very disconcerting response. Somewhat tearful, I asked my OB about postpartum depression, and she announced confidently that I just needed more sleep. (Here is where I note that even doctors sometimes get it wrong.) While that was certainly true, it was not the only issue. This response proved to be a major roadblock for me, because I placed a lot of trust in my doctor.

A few months later, during which my symptoms had continued to worsen, I sought treatment from a psychiatrist who specialized in women's depression. She was a wonderful resource and directed me to my therapist, who has helped me in more ways than she will ever know. I was nursing my son at that point, and I resisted medication for a long time because I truly enjoyed the experience of breastfeeding my child. Treatment for PPD has many facets, and I was adamant that going on medication at that point would not be one of them. I started regular therapy sessions and began to exercise again, something I had always loved. These steps helped to some extent, but I still struggled. After my son celebrated his first birthday, I decided I would give medication a try and was completely surprised at its effect. I felt that a weight on my soul had been lifted. After a few months, I felt like myself in the best sense.

By the time I turned thirty-seven, I had recovered from the PPD, and I emerged oddly stronger than ever. In fact, I was glad to be in my late thirties. The only problem was that conquering PPD meant doing things that were still looked down upon. Celebrities were battling in the news about whether taking antidepressants was a good thing, and the rest of society was right there with them. People still speak in hushed terms about the need for something to take the edge off. Experts continue to opine. Are we too drugged up? Are our lives too complicated, making us all need Prozac? I have no idea what the answer is. I do know that complete treatment of my depression has made me—surprisingly enough—a pillar of strength. I'm comfortable in my own skin, and I actually have the confidence and ability to lead people (and not just the small ones who live with me).

A few years after my horrible experience with PPD, I was having dinner with a few of those same lovely ladies, and we were talking about the fact that we were all turning thirty-eight, thirty-nine, and yes, forty.

"I'm glad to be this age," I told them. And I am. I feel I've come into myself. I don't have to apologize for who I am, and I have so much to offer. It turns out that I still love to sing and have joined a classical singing chorale. Also, I had fun (seriously) running our school's parent-teacher organization, and I love to have a house full of boys running to and fro in my neighborhood. I'm still a mess. That hasn't changed, which will surprise none of my close friends, but it's like my husband said the other day: "You like living in chaos and having a lot going on with our kids." And it's true.

At this point in my life, I feel capable and grateful and thankful. I imagine this must be what those without depression feel like on their good days. With treatment, both physical and mental, I have come into myself again. Wrestling with depression is not daily anymore, although I do think about this condition often. I feel grateful to be where I am with my family. I still miss my dad every day, and my children are my delight—and my torment, if we are being honest. My third son is such a great boy, but when he has issues, I still blame myself and the PPD, which brings me to my therapist, who helps me deal with my guilt and other remaining issues.

I do know that the posters in doctors' offices advising women to call about postpartum depression are a very good thing. We need to be our own advocate, which is tremendously difficult when you can barely keep it together to get to a doctor in the first place. But if your health professional shrugs off your issues the way mine did, seek another opinion. Your doctor could be a great doctor, like mine, but not great at mental health. I often wish I could tell my younger self to see a counselor. My therapist saw me for six months before I even considered medication, and it helped. Just not enough. It was good for me to realize that.

Depression doesn't happen because a person is weak. It is a chemical imbalance in the brain. For some of us, medication is needed to help push the reset button. It is not an easy way out; sometimes it is the only way out. Therapy is the other equally or even more important aspect. Seeking help is the way to health. Recognizing the need for treatment and sticking with it can bring the return of normalcy and even joy.

As for the benefits of being forty, I will say this: with age comes experience and wisdom. My younger self fought the idea of having anything wrong for so long. She delayed and procrastinated and filled her life with busy work to hide the pain. In the end, I'm a much better person for having finally admitted I couldn't just wish it or wait it away. I sought help, and if you have any of those same feelings, I hope you will, too.

Last week, my grandmother, whom I am still very close to, asked me if I would go back to my college days. The answer is a resounding no. I lived it—some of it was wonderful and some of it terrible. But I'm far stronger and more content now than I ever was then. I'm living on my own terms as the woman I was meant to be. I'm a bit of a late bloomer in this regard, but the journey has been so worth it.

Anne Karrick Scott Deetsch is a full-time stay-at-home mother with four children, a husband, a dog, and several fish. She cooks with abandon and embraces her disorganized life.

CHAPTER 7

ON HOPE:
TURNING A DEATH SENTENCE INTO A LIFE WELL LIVED

By Heather Von St. James

"When hope is in the equation, the odds don't matter." Those were the words my surgeon told me twelve days after my life had turned upside down. On November 21, 2005, at 1:30 p.m., I got the news that everyone fears most: "You have cancer."

I was diagnosed with malignant pleural mesothelioma, an insidious cancer caused by asbestos. My father, a man who worked in drywall construction, had unknowingly exposed me to asbestos through his work jacket.

I sat there in utter shock...cancer. Okay, but the severity of the type of cancer I had was far more shocking than the diagnosis—the survival rate was 2 percent. My first thought was: I've just had a baby, and now *this*?

My doctor told me that if I did nothing, I would be lucky to live fifteen months. The bottom dropped out of my world. All I could think about was my three-month-old baby girl at home—not the cancer. Here I was, a new mom, and I was being given a death sentence. More than anything, I desperately needed hope.

When I was given my diagnosis, I was told I had three options. I could do nothing and live maybe fifteen months. I could do chemo and radiation and maybe live five years. Or I could have a mostly experimental surgery done by a specialist in the field of mesothelioma and probably, if things went well, get up to ten years.

The third option had a couple of drawbacks. First, the surgery involved the removal of my entire left lung. Second, the surgeon was located in Boston, 1,400 miles from my home in Minnesota. Without missing a beat, my husband said, "Get us to Boston."

Twelve days later, there we were at Brigham and Women's Hospital in Boston, sitting in an orientation with other mesothelioma patients. I learned a lot about mesothelioma that day. I learned that I was much younger than the average patient. I learned that the disease usually develops ten to forty years after exposure to asbestos. I also learned that there is no cure and that it is terminal. Over 90 percent of patients diagnosed don't live beyond eighteen months.

It was on that day that Dr. David Sugarbaker said that comforting phrase to me and with those words gave me the hope I so desperately needed. He gave me something to hold on to—the hope that I would be around to see my baby girl grow up. He also instilled in me a desire to never give up.

After days of tests and biopsies, we learned that I was a perfect candidate for the surgery. It would mean the removal of my entire left lung and the lining around the lung where the tumor was. Dr. Sugarbaker would also take the left half of my diaphragm and the lining around my heart, replacing those with surgical Gore-Tex. One or two ribs would also have to be removed to allow space to work in the chest cavity. During the surgery, a heated chemotherapy solution would be pumped into my chest, washed around for an hour, and then pumped out. To say I was nervous would be an understatement, but I trusted Dr. Sugarbaker, and I held on to hope.

My surgery took place on February 2, 2006, and on February 2, 2017, I celebrated eleven years of being cancer-free, and the hope Dr. Sugarbaker instilled in me is still alive and well.

I've spent much of the last eleven years working as a patient advocate, fighting for the rights of asbestos victims, and educating people about the disease through my blog. I've had the honor of meeting and working with people who find themselves in the same position I was in eleven years ago: diagnosed with a rare cancer, being told they only have months to live, and then going online and reading more horrific statistics about the disease and losing any hope they had. I do all I can to instill in them the hope that I found. My wish for them is that they will say, "If she can survive it, I can too."

I have found cancer survivors to be some of the most real and down-to-earth people I've ever met. We call a spade a spade and don't waste our time on petty things. We live our lives with a different viewpoint than most. Some call it living for today and others living in the moment. I call it being real. I find that in friendships, I'm much pickier about whom I spend time with and whom I make friends with. I don't have time for people who don't bring into my life something positive. Cancer gave me a clarity that I'd never had before and the ability to weed out the toxic people in my life. There were people I tried sharing my hope for a better life with, but due to their own inability to see all that life has to offer, they only wanted to be around me to emotionally bleed me dry. I weeded these people out and now have friends around me who share my mind-set. The older I have gotten, the easier this has been. It is a sort of freedom that comes as you age. I share with new friends the hope for a bright future, and it is contagious.

Some people see hope as a waste of time and energy. It's not tangible, so why put your energy into something that is not a given? When your life is shattered and the very foundation you built everything on is ripped out from underneath you, two things remain: faith and hope. They go hand in hand. No, not tangible, but something internal that drives you during times when you just want to give up.

My body has endured so much. First, there was the surgery. Following it, I had four sessions of chemo that left me weak and frail. I then had to go through thirty sessions of radiation that all but destroyed any strength I had left. I lost almost a hundred pounds. My left side has an incision scar that wraps around the side of my body from under my breast to below my shoulder blade. My left hand is numb, and I sweat on only half of my body. I get winded going up stairs or steep inclines, and my stamina is not what it used to be. I lost my career due to the cancer, a career I loved and at which I excelled.

Cancer took a lot from me. But you know what else it did? It strengthened my faith in a higher power and in myself. It made me realize that I am stronger than I ever imagined and that I can make it through most anything. In those times when I wanted to give up, all I had to do was look at my baby girl and remember my doctor's words. I had hope. I had hoped I would be around to raise her. I had hoped I would be around to celebrate Christmases, birthdays, and all those first milestones that come with children. Most of all, I had hoped I would be there for all the regular stuff— tucking her in at night, playing a game with her, talking in the car on the way to the mall—all those little things that make up life. That is what I really hoped for, and here I am.

When I found out I had mesothelioma, I could easily have given up after reading the statistics on the disease. The survival rate was dismal at 2 percent. That's not very encouraging to read when you are diagnosed with a disease. Instead of giving up, though, I made up my mind that someone had to be in that 2 percent—and that someone was going to be me.

My daughter is eleven years old now, and I'm an eleven-year sur-vivor. It's been an amazing journey, and I still live by those words my doctor said to me all those years ago: "When hope is in the equation, the odds don't matter." I truly believe that, and I plan on being around for many more years to come.

⇒⊰⊹⊱⇐

Heather Von St. James is a courageous mother, wife, and survivor of meso-thelioma. She has made it her mission to help other mesothelioma victims around the globe and can be found sharing her story and her message of hope at http://www.mesothelioma.com/heather/survivor/#intro.

CHAPTER 8

ON MOTHERHOOD:
TAKING THE LONG VIEW FROM UNDER THE BIG TOP

By Barbara Fleck

I have a confession to make. My child was a biter—the kind that left kids in her wake with teeth marks and tearstained cheeks. Her reign of terror lasted about six months between the ages of one and two. She didn't hit or kick or push. Her biting wasn't even particularly aggressive. In fact, I'm fairly certain that at times it was simply her way of saying hello. It was unpredictable and consistent at the same time; we never knew who she would claim as her next victim, or why, but it would always happen at day care, and it was nearly every day. She was eventually expelled. At the time, I was pretty sure it was going to go on her permanent record.

Before I had kids, I was confident I could do a better job of disciplining my children than most of the parents I saw. I had been working with kids for a while, first in recreation programs and then at a children's hospital. I saw all the behaviors and all the parental reactions, and I just knew I would take those experiences and raise perfectly respectful, obedient children. Now that I am a mother, I have a word for people of similar convictions: nonparents.

I never imagined I would be the parent of a dreaded biter. If my precious offspring ever dared attempt something so barbaric and malicious, I would simply nip that in the bud with a firm voice and sound reasoning, followed by either a timeout or redirection, and that would be that. Until, of course, it actually happened to me. We tried everything. Timeouts, negative consequences for biting, positive rewards for not biting, rational discussions, bribery, and desperate pleas, but none of those things worked.

That is how, one day, I found myself sitting on the concrete outside my daughter's day care, having just walked out for the last time with my adorable little miscreant and sobbing into her sweet-smelling hair, saying, "Why would you do this?" All the while, I was thinking, "Why would you do this...to me?"

You see, that is my *real* confession. Not that my child was a biter but that every time I got the news of her biting, I worried about what that said about me. What could the other parents be thinking about me? What kind of horrible, inattentive, incapable mother did they imagine I was? What about the day-care employees? Did they think I let her run wild at home? Or worse, that she was acting out aggression I had shown her? Everyone knows that biting is the worst toddler offense. I'd heard it on the playground when other moms would chat about one of their little darlings perhaps hitting or pushing out of frustration. "Well, at least he's not a biter," one would say, the response to which invariably was, "Yes, thank God!" Only mine *was* a biter. And in my eyes at least, that meant that I was *that* mom.

I drove home that fateful afternoon in a somber mood. Although I went through all the usual motions that make up a toddler's afternoon (putting her down for a nap, fixing a snack, playing outside, calming her meltdown, etc.), inside I felt like I was in mourning. How could this be happening? I'd read all the books, limited her screen time, reinforced good behavior, and modeled appropriate manners. What was I doing wrong? I could not let it go. When it was finally bedtime and I got the chance to talk it out with my husband, I still had not come up with any answers. He said something that at the time I took to be a cop-out. It was a joke to cheer me up and as far from helpful as possible. He said, "Don't worry about it! She probably won't still be biting people when she goes to college." All my thirty-year-old self could think was, "That doesn't fix it *now!*"

What happened next was not particularly surprising. I delivered my second child a week later, and since I was home anyway, we did not look for a new day care. With my firstborn no longer in day care, the only place the biting had ever occurred, the problem stopped. I can honestly say I had nothing to do with its ending, because nothing I did had ever worked. I never even got the self-righteous pleasure of saying, "There, I fixed it. I fixed *her*. I *am* a good mother." Twelve years later, I still don't know why she starting biting to begin with. I don't even care, because I've realized a few things about motherhood now that I'm in my forties.

The first thing I realized is that this is not a short-term project. We are in this for the long haul. My husband's comment that fateful night was actually pretty spot on. (And I will even admit it!) My daughter will not go to college still biting people. In fact, she didn't even go to preschool still biting people. Although at the time it felt like a major trauma that went on forever, like most things in childhood, it was short-lived. It did not develop into a major personality disorder, and it did not limit her future potential. It didn't even go on her permanent record. Our family laughs about it now, and she laughs the hardest, because it's so surprising to think of her as being that naughty. She is generally regarded as a well-behaved preteen with decent manners and lots of friends. Nary a bite mark in sight.

Had I been able to peer into the future and see that, would I have been so worried about her biting stage? Would I have tried every possible "cure" so desperately? Probably not. I like to think I would have patiently waited it out, knowing that it would pass—and in the knowing, would not have had to worry about whether other moms thought badly of me, because it would have been over soon enough.

I watch in fascination the interactions between my sister-in-law, who became a mother for the first time at thirty-nine, and her daughter. I see so many differences in the way she handles things from the way I handled my kids when I was ten years younger. I am not surprised to see that she is more patient than I was (never my strong suit, even on my best days), but I am surprised at how far that patience extends. There is no eager rush for her child to reach the next milestone or prove herself to be better than her peers. The response to any misbehavior from my niece (trust me, there is plenty—she is a typical three-year-old) is invariably met with the same gentle discussion of why that is not appropriate or redirection to a more acceptable activity. She takes the long view, thinking of the adult she would like her daughter to grow into rather than worrying too much about the kid she will be next week. No way could I have been that kind of mother when my kids were younger—mostly because I was so much younger myself. I hadn't learned to take the long view yet, to see that most of this was just a phase and that she would not still be biting in college. Now I see it.

The second realization took a little longer to come by. It has ever so slowly dawned on me that there is indeed more than one way to raise a child. Those parents I used to scoff at and assure myself I would never be like? I have been them more times than I care to admit! I have found myself hissing at my children through gritted teeth while they were fighting with each other in line at Starbucks. I have chased them down the aisles of Target. I know they have been those obnoxious kids running around the airport, tripping people up as they zoom by. My kids aren't perfect. No amount of perfect mothering is likely to make them so—which is good, because I'm not a perfect mother. No one is.

As a mother in my thirties, I spent a lot of time comparing my kids to other kids and thus myself to other moms. Were my kids smarter than their classmates? Did they have more friends? Were they less polite? Did they get into more trouble? I think that's a natural part of parenthood in some ways. But I also spent a lot of time wondering what I was like as a mother compared to other moms. Was I too strict? Too lenient? Nurturing enough? So-and-so's daughter was always so kind to others…what was she doing that I wasn't? I spent way too much time and energy trying to answer questions I probably shouldn't have been asking myself to begin with, and I'm pretty sure this inner monologue was the beginning of my gray hair and wrinkles.

Advancing age brought with it certain revelations. Our kids are all different. *We* are all different. Is it any wonder that no two parent-child combinations are the same? Can we really expect that the way one unique adult disciplines another unique child will work equally well for a completely different pair? Crazy talk. Let's face it—we are all just winging it. We try what we think will work based on what we know about our kids. Sometimes it does. Sometimes it doesn't. Comparing how I'm doing it to how another mom is doing it is like comparing apples to orangutans. I finally had to just stop. I had to recognize that we are all doing this parenting thing the best way we know how, and we are all getting it right and messing it up equally. Plus, I don't need any extra help developing gray hairs or wrinkles. I now have a new inner monologue, which is actually an old Polish proverb: Not my circus; not my monkeys. How other moms deal with their kids has no bearing on me and mine. That's a whole different circus, after all.

I hear a lot of my friends in their forties talking about how much more comfortable they feel in their own skin. They are unapologetic about who they are and confident in their opinions and capabilities. This is certainly becoming true for me, and I feel that this extends to motherhood as well. Am I confident that I am doing the right thing as a mother at all times? Of course not! But I *am* sure that I am raising my children well and that no one else could do a better job. They are *my* kids, *my* circus, *my* monkeys. I know them better than anyone else, so why would I compare myself to other moms who don't have my kids? Better still, why would I worry about what others think of my parenting now when I am focused on helping my kids develop into meaningful human beings in the long run?

Striving to focus on the long run in the battles with my children often has me looking back on my own childhood. I know I had many of the same battles with my mother. I remember thinking that she had no idea who I really was or what was truly important to a kid. With every passing year, my mother seemed to get more and more clueless. That is, of course, until I had children, at which point I recognized her brilliance. She managed to stay unwavering in her parenting of me through all the volatility of my youth and adolescence, consistently focusing on the same values of hard work, responsibility, and kindness. When I erred in any of these areas, she seemed disappointed but not surprised. She expected I would make mistakes from time to time, but she did not dwell on them. I know she was taking the long view, as she often told me that it wasn't her job to make me like her but to make me into an independent woman. I like to think that she did her job very well!

Remember that earlier confession I made, the real one, where I said I worried about what my daughter's behavior said about me? Well, I won't say that I no longer have these thoughts in my forties. But they arise much less often. Frankly, that question is just not that important anymore. Once I had these brilliant revelations—that there is no one right way and no one wrong way to raise kids and that parenting is a long-term proposition—it became less about me and more about them. My concerns now are about what their behavior is telling me about their emotions, about their perceptions of the world around them. I hope my interactions with them are helping them grow into responsible people. Isn't that the end goal for all of us?

Flash forward ten or so years from that day in the day-care parking lot. I am now a substitute teacher at my daughter's school. One day, I was approached in the hall by the music teacher, who was a bit embarrassed to have to tell me what had happened in class earlier. It seems my daughter had let her impulsivity get the better of her and, a little less than playfully, had punched a boy in the stomach. The teacher was struggling with what to do, since she did not witness the incident and my daughter had not previously been in trouble. Perhaps she was thinking I would prefer to handle it at home and was giving me the courtesy she would give another colleague in a similar situation. I didn't really consider this at the time. What I did consider was that my child likely knew that what she had done was wrong and, since consequences were not immediately forthcoming, was sitting in her regular classroom thinking one of two things. Either she was thinking, "Yes! I didn't get in trouble, and he clearly deserved it!" Or, more likely, "Man, they are going to drop the bomb on me soon, and I'll be in really, really big trouble!" Neither of those things seemed fair to me.

I told the teacher I would rather my daughter receive whatever consequences normally apply in this case, that same day if possible. I wondered what kind of effect this might have on my daughter's view of school. I wondered what her future interactions with this boy would be like. I thought about how I would handle the discussion about this when we got home. Not once did I consider whether the teachers involved would think poorly of me because of this. Of course, their opinion of me mattered, but I was confident that I was doing the right thing for my child, and I knew they saw that her actions in this instance were nothing more than that—the actions of an instance, not her underlying character. Since it is that underlying character that I'm investing my time in, that is what matters in the long run.

So, along with the wrinkles and gray hairs, the arrival of my forties has brought me an added bonus: the long view. It is both the ability to look back and see where I came from and the ability to look forward toward the ultimate goal. I am certainly not the master of motherhood yet, as my children will surely attest, but I *have* mastered the art of taking the long view. I've learned to embrace the good *and* the bad, and—most importantly—to always remember that moms are not just moms; they are also ringmasters of their very own circuses. And while the mom circus may have its ups and downs (and biters and hitters and jugglers, too), I can't deny that it really is the greatest show on earth.

━≼┼≽━

Barbara Fleck is a mom of two, who recently stopped using her fancy science degree to pursue a less stressful job as a substitute teacher…an illusion that lasted until the first indoor recess. She continues to substitute because she enjoys interacting with people her own mental age—and because she spends less money if she is at school all day.

CHAPTER 9

ON GROWING UP BLACK AND WHITE IN AMERICA:
HOW I LEARNED TO LIVE MY LIFE BOLDLY IN MY OWN UNIQUE WAY

By Elizabeth Pendleton

I 'm half of a half of a half of a half...so what am I? Living in an ambiguous space in America, that's what.

Growing up, I was too black for the white kids and too white for the black kids. Or was I? Perception was the name of the game. Apologizing or not committing to what I thought people wanted me to be is the very state I lived in—and the very state I still struggle to climb out of. And whose perception was it? Theirs? Mine? It is a constant journey.

Once when I was a kid, a little white girl came up to me and asked, "What are you?"

"What do you mean?" I asked.

"Black or white?" she replied.

To her, it was as simple as that. Nothing else existed. When I asked her what she meant, she repeated her question. "Black or white?" I told her I was both, but she wasn't having any of it.

Adamantly she told me, "No you aren't. You just want to be friends with everybody."

Had I been older and wiser, I would have asked what was so wrong about wanting to be friends with everybody, but at the time, I was just in first grade—and super confused. I remember saying, "No, you can come home and see my parents."

That was the beginning of incredible confusion for me. I took everything to heart and somehow, being very hard on myself, I figured it was something I needed to fix. The question was how? You live inside yourself, so you can't wash, peel, or erase away anything that's on the outside. You are who you are—black, white, brown, or purple.

Now that I think of it, it must have been on my radar way earlier than I even realized. I remember having a black boyfriend and a white boyfriend in preschool...you know, to be fair and all. And I made Father's Day cards for my dad on Mother's Day and Mother's Day cards on Father's Day so that neither would feel left out and all would be fair. It was a lifetime of trying to do what was fair to everyone else. And let's not forget trying to be perfect. I just knew that if I were perfect, then there would be no reason for others not to like me. So, I became a master at reading what others needed and presenting that persona to them. I was terrified of getting too close to anyone, because I didn't know if I could sustain being a fraud. What *I* needed never factored into what *they* needed, so my opinion on most things was an observation of what others' opinions were. That was what came out of my mouth. It never even entered my mind that deep down I might not agree with it. If I were to survive, there wasn't time for that. And that's what it felt like: surviving.

Now, all that sounds very extreme. It was, and it wasn't. It was a very quick formula to live the easiest way possible—at least, that's how I saw it through my kid lens at the time. Being an all-or-nothing personality, I went all in.

So, let's look at the time. I was born in June 1967—a few months before the anti-miscegenation laws were overturned by the Supreme Court in the *Loving vs. Virginia* case. My dad, who is black, had just moved back to Virginia (from Massachusetts), where he'd waited on the ruling before bringing my mom and me out to live with him. The times were charged. I was an infant. Infants don't talk, but they absorb everything, especially tension and joy in the air.

The police pulled my parents over and asked my white mom if she was okay. The community pool asked to see us first before letting us join. At shopping centers or on road trips, people would stare. My dad, super quick, would bound up to them all smiles and ask how they were—as if they'd previously met and hit it off. It confused the hell out of them. But here's the best one—my parents' first house was sold to them out of revenge. That's right. The owner hated his neighbors so much that he thought he'd get back at them by bringing "those people" into the neighborhood. He even left my parents a gun in case they "needed to protect themselves." We lived there eleven years. No gun was needed, but our stay wasn't seamless.

Right off the bat, my parents went to the ongoing neighborhood bridge game, only to have no one show up but the hosts. The hosts became good friends. Civil-rights groups checked in on my parents, offering help and desperately wanting them to succeed.

It was during this time that my dad got a call from a newspaper reporter wanting to interview him and my mom about their marriage. It went something like this:

"Why?" asked my dad when he got the call.

"Because we want to write about the typical biracial marriage."

"What's that typical marriage look like?" my dad asked.

"Well, you know," the reporter said. "The wife is an ex-stripper and the husband an ex-con."

The reporter was actually serious. My dad hung up.
Click.

Both my parents were highly educated. One of the founders of Yale was a relative of my mom's, and while my dad had come out of one of the area's roughest neighborhoods, he'd skipped several grades and had wonderful mentors who guided him on his road to becoming a university professor. He is black—black and eleven years older than my mom. He experienced a lot, and he wanted life to be as easy as possible for me. He wanted me to blend in and accentuate my white aspects. I couldn't wear my hair down and curly because it made me look too black. Survive. His approach wasn't based on perception; it was based on a hard life and real experiences. My time was easier than his. His reaction was based on the reality of his time. As was—and is—mine. So, back to mine…

I chose a big university in order to get lost in the crowd. I always preferred hanging out with several people over a few, although I did find some very good and trusted friends along the way. I never had a boyfriend until college—never even went on a date. I didn't get asked to my prom, although in hindsight, I was good-looking—or I must have had *some* beauty shining through, since I went on to be a model. I had the perfect "white" nose, but after seeing *Roots*, I would lie in bed for hours, praying my lips would shrink. The irony isn't lost on me that my lips ended up being one of my best features.

Every slight felt like an arrow to me, reminding me that I was not enough. It all stemmed back to the question of what standard I was trying to measure myself against. I didn't seem to fit anywhere.

By nature, I was a brave kid. Throughout my life, I've done very spontaneous, bold things. That quality has never left me. In middle school, I took a test to see what language I should study. It said none, so I signed up for two. And at fifteen, unbeknownst to my parents, I signed myself up for a German exchange program. They found out at the school open house. And I still went.

My superpower was being able to disappear completely into any crowd, likely achieved by never really revealing much about myself. I felt safe in that anonymity, and it has affected everything I've done. In college, my desire not to label myself annoyed some black students who wanted to start a black phone book. It was the same with black sororities. And white ones, for that matter. Blend, disappear—that was the name of the game. Don't define.

That started to change right after college. I was modeling—a profession in which my looks were constantly being scrutinized. The blending got harder, and the merging got messy. Which part of me would win?

These separate parts wound up watering each other down, which resulted in my being an inconsistent model. On a shoot, one minute I'd be brave and bold and do a good job, and the next I'd crumble and disappear under the scrutiny. I'd get great representation and then be terrified to go in and keep up the relationship for fear that the more they got to know me, they'd start thinking they'd made a terrible mistake. The bold kid in me was saying, "HERE I AM!" and the shell-shocked one was a deer in the headlights.

Claiming my self-worth and standing tall in who I am is the boulder I still push up the hill. Now, as a personal trainer in Los Angeles, I'll find myself training a high-profile client and starting out great, only to then panic, wondering if I can keep it up on subsequent visits. Sometimes I can, and sometimes I can't. It makes me so mad, because intellectually I think I've gotten beyond that insecurity, but emotionally it's still a stumbling block.

While modeling, I lived in Holland and saw many people of mixed race my age and older. My mouth was agape, as I saw these were actually appreciated, desired people. A trip that had started as just a stopover on my way to somewhere else became three-plus years. The freedoms I saw there took root in my soul and lay there bubbling in wait. Then, while on vacation in Kenya, I saw local black men who were just like white men back here in the United States. They owned the ground they walked on. There was no heaviness at being perceived as a thug. There was no wondering if the person who'd just crossed the street was thinking it might be safer on the other side. I only recognized these things by their contrast with my own reality. I was amazed. Finally, my unconscious perception shifted. It was more food for thought but also a message that was as clear as day. It made me wonder, Who am I?

I knew I had a lot going for me. I knew I was a good reader of people and could enjoy life's adventures and have a lot of fun with them. I was a kind person and didn't want people to feel unwanted.

I moved back to the United States just before turning thirty. I started consciously and experimentally voicing my opinions. I'd give my opinion about a movie I had seen...*before* hearing someone else's opinion. I also tried to honor those times I didn't want to say anything, choosing not to fill in the space like the Happy Hostess—a nickname I had given myself in my twenties as I tried to be that perfect person. That's much bigger than you can ever imagine. To me, anonymity was comfortable.

Anonymous, I traveled the world, lived as a local, had wonderful experiences, and was nonplussed at being alone. One-on-one encounters required a much more focused effort. I was now spending more personal time with other people and struggling to share my imperfect parts with them. I don't know—maybe a lot of people are like that. What I do know is that I did a lot of work in my thirties to overcome the impact of the things impressed upon me as a kid. Those things are ingrained in you, and I'm still working to vanquish mine.

Luckily, some great people slipped through my defenses during this journey—including great boyfriends, who always surprised me by believing in me and valuing me, and a few truly amazing people who became trusted and lifelong friends. Getting to my husband and that level of letting someone in has taken slow but steady growth. These people all helped shape the woman I am today, and they continue to help pave the way.

In my forties, I've got great relationships across the board, even though my emotional fears of not being good enough aren't completely a thing of the past. I still try to be perfect, but I channel this toward more productive things like honing my craft—always, always taking classes and getting certifications that help my work. I'm not the best at confrontation. In fact, I'm pretty messy at it; it causes me a tremendous amount of anxiety. But I do it anyway in order to speak my truth and to honor myself. That's life, right? We can only get so far before it gets uncomfortable, and then we have to face our fears. We have to keep doing our reveals—to ourselves and to others—and we have to keep on persevering. It's my onion being peeled away from the inside out, layer by layer, year after year. The irony is that it's a lifelong challenge we all face from the get-go—whether we're black or white or something else, we define ourselves by living our lives boldly and brilliantly in our own unique way and in our own unique skin.

So be bold. Be kind. Be true to yourself, and be open to looking beyond. People are just people, after all.

⇒⊣⊢⇐

Elizabeth Pendleton is a working mother of a three-year-old wild child. No, it's not her grandchild. She's realizing that like it or not, her body has no choice but to keep up with the physical prowess of her budding track star/ parkour extraordinaire and that any memory loss is OBVIOUSLY due to sleep deprivation (which her sister failed to really warn her about before motherhood).

CHAPTER 10

ON SURVIVING BREAST CANCER:
HOW THE BOOBS YOU LOVE AND THE FOOTBALL YOU DON'T ALL COME TOGETHER IN THE END

By Emily Cooke

Like most women I know, I have had body issues most of my life. I have never liked my chin, I found flaws with my tummy, and my butt has been a source of disappointment for years. But I have always loved one part of my body: my breasts. I've always thought they were perfect. They are big (but not too big), firm and high, round and heavy. Other people thought they were perfect, too. Trust me, people have commented! Looking in the mirror, I could overlook the other unflattering bits (butt, thighs, tummy, etc.) and always see my best asset—my perfect breasts! In college, when I was young and fresh, I was a nude model for art classes. I was proud of my body—especially my gorgeous breasts. Even now, in my forties—with age and after breastfeeding two babies—they were still awesome.

Then, one day, I found out they were not perfect. One day, I found out I had breast cancer.

It started innocently enough with my annual mammogram. I truly believe getting a mammogram is the right thing to do, and while it is horribly uncomfortable, I went every year after turning forty. I never liked going, and I was always nervous, because no matter how important I knew it was to have my checkup, there was always the fear that I would hear bad news. I think that is why so many women avoid getting their mammograms—no one ever wants to get *that* news.

I don't even remember that fateful mammogram, since it was such a routine exam. I'm sure I made inappropriate jokes with the technician, as I tend to do when I am nervous and seminude. About a week after that mammogram, a letter arrived in the mail with what I thought were the routine results. I remember reading it with a blasé attitude. I was in the kitchen getting ready to make dinner for my kids, and I picked it up and pretended to read it out loud, saying, "Blah blah blah, nothing to report, come back next year." Unfortunately, it said something more like, "Inconclusive results…need to retest…please make a new appointment as soon as possible."

I had received something like this once before, so my concern meter was high but not freaking-out high. I went back in for more images, and then, when they needed more information, they did a sonogram of my left breast. Apparently they saw something that raised concerns. The doctor and his technician were trying to be easygoing with their demeanor, but I think you can always tell when something is not quite right and they aren't allowed to tell you. Their mannerisms change; they seem uncomfortable and get weirdly quiet or make stupid small talk.

They recommended a biopsy, but being the conservative patient, I opted for a second opinion. The second doctor suggested a biopsy as well. I was still concerned at this point but not yet completely freaking out. I kept telling myself that it was wasted energy to worry about something until I knew for certain.

The biopsy was a fiasco. During the procedure, the doctor punctured a blood vessel and created a hematoma. This hematoma was huge! Not only did my breast hurt from being biopsied, it was also black and blue. In my effort to be funny, again seminude, I told the technician that the doctor had ruined my dating life until the hematoma healed. Yes, that's me, the seminude, nervous woman making inappropriate jokes.

When it was time for the consultation to get the results, I sat on the exam table in my paper gown waiting for the breast specialist. Why I had to get into a paper gown to hear the results is still a mystery to me, but there I sat with my paper gown soaked through. I think the term is "flop sweat."

That was when I heard that my left breast had a tumor. Not a huge tumor, but a tumor nonetheless.

What? Not me! Not my perfect boobs!

I began to cry, and the doctor handed me a paper towel to wipe my tears. Gee, thanks for your stellar bedside manner, doc. Not even a box of tissues? It seemed a fitting precursor to what would be a bumpy ride.

Luckily, I had a friend who had already gone through the breast-cancer thing and gave me a referral for a surgeon. (Yes, I felt lucky to have a friend who had already survived breast cancer who could give me a personal referral.) At first, they thought I was going to have a lumpectomy, where they take out the mass and leave the boob as intact as possible. I thought that was a decent proposal and was on board and relatively calm. I soon found out that I had several other "suspicious" masses that might be cancerous. With this news, the lumpectomy was off the table. I was told I needed a mastectomy, and before I knew it, I was shopping for boobs. As my ex-boyfriend astutely noted, this would allow me to combine two of my favorite things: my breasts and shopping. What more could a shopaholic ask for? The problem was, I thought the breasts I already had were perfect. I never wanted to change them, so I didn't really want to shop for a new one.

I also never liked the way implants look. To me, they almost always looked fake. So, as I began my shopping adventure, I was more than a little nervous. I set up meetings with two of the plastic surgeons my breast surgeon worked with. I felt bad for the first plastic surgeon I met. She was doing a fine job of explaining the procedure and the process, but when I found out what was involved, I lost it. First came the surgery to remove the breast, which would then be followed by the construction of the implant. They would begin by putting in "spacers" to create room to add the implant. Then, over several weeks, they would increase the spacers to the right size. I would go back several times to have more fluid injected to achieve the proper size.

I was not prepared for that. I had assumed it would all happen at once, and I would be done. I sobbed. I wept. I destroyed another paper gown with sweat and tears. Not only did the whole process completely freak me out, but none of the before-and-after photos looked good enough for my perfect breasts. To me, they looked fake, like porn-star boobs, and I fled her office as fast as I could.

I was going down the same path with the next plastic surgeon (paper gown, sweat, disappointment) when he mentioned something called the DIEP flap procedure. This was something I had heard about but not something I wanted to discuss. It involved creating a breast out of my belly fat. Now, that sounds pretty good, right? But the surgery was much longer and more intense than getting implants, and since this would be the first major surgery I'd ever had, I was scared and wanted to take the "easier" way out.

We had been looking at his before-and-after photos of breast implants, and because I was whining so much, he stopped and told me that if I wanted my new boob to look like my current one, I would have to do the DIEP flap. I appreciated his honesty and asked to see his before-and-after photos of patients who had gone with the DIEP flap. When he showed them to me, I was floored! Real boobs! I think I said, "Shit. That's what I want." Remember my issues with my body? Well, I'd never liked my belly. After the kids, it was a mess. In fact, my youngest daughter called it my "jelly belly" and would pat it and jiggle it when she sat with me or lay in bed with me. Here was a surgeon who was going to take it and make a new boob out of it. If I had to have a mastectomy, at least I could get a tummy tuck at the same time!

After we decided this was the best approach for me, the surgeon told me I might not have enough belly fat to make a breast the right size. Thankfully, he was wrong. I totally had enough of a jelly belly for a full-sized boob. We set the date for surgery.

Through the initial phase, I was straightforward with my daughters about having cancer. I wanted them to know what was happening and to be included in the whole ordeal. It was going to be scary for all of us, but I didn't want them to think talking about it or asking questions was taboo. As I prepared for the surgery, I told them I was going to be taking my belly and making a boob out of it. My youngest cried. She told me she did not want me to lose my jelly belly, that I would be a different mommy without it. She even asked if the doctor could take fat from other parts of my body like my legs instead of my belly *Wait a minute*, I thought, *she thinks I have fat legs!*

The surgeries for the mastectomy and reconstruction went well, and both procedures were done the same day. I was in surgery for around twelve hours, and most of that time was spent on the reconstruction. I remember being in the ICU the day after surgery and offering to show my new boob to anyone and everyone who came into the room. Doctors, nurses, friends, family, janitors—you name it! From the moment I saw my new boob, I knew I had made the right decision. It was perfect! Okay, it looked horrible—all swollen, with a giant incision along the side—and I was on major drugs, but it was just the result I had been hoping for. In addition, as a huge surprise, I was one of the lucky ones who got to keep my nipple, so there was no need to create a new one or get a tattoo artist to create a new one. Not only did I think my breasts were perfect, I thought my nipples were pretty great, too. I had been researching a tattoo artist in Baltimore, Maryland, who was world renowned for his amazing nipple tattoos, but I was spared having to go that route and so grateful for my good luck.

The aftermath of the surgery included three drains attached to different body parts: one from my breast and two from my belly. They were disgusting. The drains were meant to draw blood and tissue from the incisions, and I don't think I have the words to describe how awful it was to see them in action. Not only was I dealing with the gross factor, I was constantly tangling myself up, and my reactions were truly unladylike, including a lot of swearing about the "effing" tubes. In addition, I had two wire-like lines coming from my belly incision that were attached to a medicine ball in a zippered pouch that continuously dosed me with pain medication. I was a mess.

Another special post-op treat was that I could not stand up straight—I had to walk hunched over like an old woman with a bad case of osteoporosis. For decades, I had been told to stand up straight, but now I was required to hunch over. I was not allowed to sleep on my side or flat on my back for six weeks.

My postsurgery journey opened my eyes to all the love that is in my life. Since I am divorced, I did not have a husband to lean on, to cry to, and to help me make decisions about the cancer treatment. However, my network of friends and family sprang into action, and I was overwhelmed by their love and support. By the time I got home from the hospital, there was a La-Z-Boy recliner in my living room for me to sleep in for the next few weeks, a full schedule of lunches and dinners for the following two weeks, and a slew of flowers, cards, and visitors.

My sister had volunteered to be my nurse for the first week after surgery, as I was not allowed to be alone. She had the pleasure of learning how to strip my drains (gag), measure the nastiness that came out of the drains (double gag), and help me bathe. Did I mention that she is incredibly squeamish? Somehow, when you need to step up, you can and you do. By the way, she is in her forties, too. We spent that week laughing, watching TV, and stripping drains. I wasn't very mobile, was somewhat cranky, and wasn't adept at bathing with drains hanging off my hunched-over body. She truly earned a Best Sister Award that week, and I couldn't have done it without her. She kept me smiling, she let me cry, and she slept on the couch next to me.

During my second week of recovery, I met with the oncologist for the first time. I was still uncertain about whether I would need chemotherapy. Since my surgery had gone well, I had kept my nipple, and they'd confirmed that the cancer had not yet gone to my lymph nodes, I thought I was in the clear. Unfortunately, the oncologist informed me that the cancer had micrometastasized and that I was going to need chemo—no radiation, but yes for chemo. I was stunned, but since she said *micro*metastasized, I thought I would maybe need a micro dose of chemo. Uh...no. Apparently, the treatment for a tiny bit of cancer is twenty weeks of chemo. Twenty weeks! That's five months, which to me seemed like a cruel joke.

I was devastated. I was not prepared for that news. I can't remember what happened next, but I know I had to wait for the drains to come out before starting chemo. The oncologist also explained that I would need to have a port implanted in my chest that would allow them to plug me into the machine that pumps the chemo into the body. I would be experiencing what it felt like to be a kind of human electrical outlet.

The day I went to have the port implanted, I was scared. I had just had major surgery a couple weeks before and was now going to go under again. Soon after changing into my surgery wear, the fear caught up to me, and I began to cry. The nurse told me that I needed to be brave for my kids, that they would appreciate a mom who was strong, and that it was my job to show them this was going to be okay. I told her that I agreed with her, but I added that I *had* been brave for my kids, that they *knew* I was strong, and since my kids were not even at the hospital with me, they would never know I'd cried, so I could damn well cry as much as I wanted.

Maybe it was karma for being bitchy to the nurse, but when they wheeled me into the surgery room, the speakers were blaring Queen's "Another One Bites the Dust." I am superstitious, but I usually try to keep that a secret. In this instance, I allowed my superstition to take over and asked them to change the music. No reason to tempt fate. As I was pumped full of anesthesia, drifting off into unconsciousness, I wondered: What will be next on the playlist—"Stairway to Heaven"?

Good news: I didn't die, and the port was successfully implanted. With the port, I had a big lump near my right clavicle that was going to act as an outlet where they would plug me in for chemo. I was so freaked out by it that I could barely look at it, and I definitely couldn't touch it. With the port in place, I was almost ready for chemo.

Chemo was going to happen in two different stages. First, I was scheduled to receive four treatments of the hard stuff, which some patients call "the Red Devil," and then twelve weeks of the regular chemo. But before I could even get started, I had to prep my port and my body. There were several different kinds of antinausea medications I had to take along with a bunch of other pills. I don't remember what they were, but the doctors said to take them, so I took them. Some I had to take the day *before* chemo, and some I had to take the day *of* chemo. I also had a special numbing cream that I was to put on my port at least an hour before my chemo appointment so that when they jabbed the three-inch-long needle into it, it wouldn't hurt so much. I was still grossed out about that area, and now I was forced not only to touch it but also to slather cream on it.

My chemo appointments were scheduled for Thursdays so that if I got really sick, I would only have to take Fridays off work, and I could recover over the weekend. My appointments were in the early afternoon, so I would go to work in the morning and slather on the numbing cream an hour before chemo. To add insult to injury, I had to cover it with plastic wrap so the cream didn't smear off! Yup, I walked around my office with plastic wrap on my chest.

There were a lot of rules to follow for chemo. I was required to have a buddy drive me to the first appointment and stay with me for the whole time they pumped me full of poison...er, I mean lifesaving chemo. That way, if I was sick from the treatment or reacted poorly, my buddy could drive me home. In addition to having my buddy by my side, I brought a bag full of goodies—a book, a shawl/blanket (knitted by some very loving church ladies), crossword puzzles, snacks, and water. Since this would be my first time, they didn't know how long it would take—it could be any-where from two to five hours. They could slow down the speed of the infusion if I was feeling queasy, or if I was handling it well, they could keep it at a moderate pace.

My treatment took place in my doctor's office in a separate area for chemo infusions that had a private room for each patient. These rooms were relatively small with a curtain for a door, and each room had a big, bulky, hospital-grade reclining chair and a regular chair for a guest. Also in the room was the stand they would hang the bag of chemo from as it was infused into me. There was also the obligatory box of Kleenex and a TV, but alas, there was no Wi-Fi. All the rooms had windows, though, which was nice.

I ended up having four different friends escort me for the first four chemo sessions. My chemo buddies' job was to keep me oc-cupied and entertained. I don't remember much about the first session, and in truth, they all became somewhat routine. What I do remember were the friends who came with me, the love I had for their friendship, and…my pee. During the first chemo treatments, my pee was a mixture of pink and orange, and there was a lot of it. I had not expected to pee so much during chemo. It seemed like a waste that I would pee out all the Red Devil during my sessions—it went in and then immediately came out.

The chemo nurses were amazing. I would get a different one almost every time, and they were all so nice. The process started each time with the assigned nurse collecting a sample of blood and asking some general questions before plugging me in. Then she would leave me alone for the duration. Sometimes the chemo machine would beep, and whichever nurse was available would come in to check on it and me. They never acted as though this was a horrible place, and they kept the mood light.

The question everyone asked me during the first few weeks concerned my hair. Was I going to lose it, and if so, when? My oncologist and the nurses told me that while not all chemo patients lose their hair, I would definitely lose mine. What they couldn't tell me was when. Some people told me it would be between the third and fourth chemo treatment. Some said I would feel my head buzz or tingle before it all fell out. I had already gotten myself ready with a prechemo haircut that was short and sassy. My hairdresser and I had talked during my prechemo cut about when to shave my head. She refused to let me shave my head myself, saying that it needed to be done by a professional or it would look bad.

One day between my third and fourth chemo appointments, I ran my hand through my hair, and a whole bunch of it came out. Thinking it was strange, I did it again, and another bunch of hair came out. By the time I had stopped running my fingers through it, I had another new hairdo. It was not even. It was not cute. It was awful.

Even though I had known it would happen, I was devastated. The reality was far worse than I had imagined. My girls watched as my hair came out in handfuls. Later, as I sobbed and wailed in my bed at bedtime, they were very sweet and tried to comfort me, but I was inconsolable.

The next day, I explained to my children that when I picked them up in the afternoon, I would be bald. My hairdresser was un-available until many days later, but I couldn't wait. After dropping off the kids, I stopped in at a random barber shop. When I walked in, it was clear that I was out of place.

I sat down and waited my turn behind a couple of old men. When the barber finally called me, I explained that I wanted to have my head shaved because I had cancer. He responded with a knowing nod and said he understood. He started the process, and we chatted for a bit. Then, about three minutes into the shave, I yelled "WAIT! You're not taking it *all* off, are you?" The clippers immediately stopped, and his hand pulled away from my head. I smiled a huge smile and said, "Just kidding!" The other men in the shop, who appeared to be holding their breath, laughed along with me, but I swear the barber almost cried.

I was not immediately comfortable with my new look, and my kids made me wear a hat whenever we were together. They really had a hard time with a bald mother. I tried many of the different options for covering my head. I had a bright-purple wig and two regular wigs, but after trying them all for different occasions, I found that none were fun to wear. I opted for silk scarves and ban-danas for a while, but eventually just left all the headwear behind.

While I had expected to lose all the hair on my head, I had not expected to lose all of my hair *everywhere*. I had not expected to get a temporary reprieve from shaving my legs and from bikini waxes. I had read a blog by a woman who commented on losing her eyelashes, so I was somewhat prepared for that. What no one told me was that I would also lose my nose hair. You wouldn't think that would be a big deal, but without nose hair, I had a really runny nose. Later, when my hair started growing back, it came in curly where before it had been straight, and it came in straight where before it had been curly. The reason for this will forever be a mystery to me.

I had expected to feel horrible during chemo. I have seen several movie renditions of how people react to chemo, and I expected the worst. I was very lucky in that I really never felt sick. After the first few sessions, I even stopped taking the antinausea pills. It became routine, and on the Thursdays that I had chemo, I would go to my job in the mornings, go to chemo, and then return to work in the afternoon. Twenty weeks of chemo didn't seem like the end of the world, after all.

One result of the whole ordeal I did not expect—having breast cancer got me to like football. During my chemo, I was selected by the Washington Redskins to participate in their "A Crucial Catch" program, which honors breast-cancer survivors during the month of October. Say what you will about their team name, the Redskins were really good to me. The program allowed me to go to the Redskins training facility for a luncheon and a day of pampering. During the event, our small group of survivors got to choose a free wig, have a massage, get a new pair of free Gap jeans, have our makeup done, dance to music pumped out by a live DJ, and take a tour of the facility led by the players. At the end of the day, we got a big basket of goodies, including a Redskins jersey and two tickets to an upcoming Redskins game. We were told that at the start of the game, we would be down on the field to cheer on the players as they ran out from the tunnel! For a Washington Redskins fan, this was a dream come true! But guess what? I didn't like football. My ex-husband had tried for years to get me to like it, and it had never worked. I hated football!

I was the only attendee at the "A Crucial Catch" event who was not in Redskins gear. I didn't know any of the players' names except Robert Griffin III and had not planned on asking for autographs. In short, I was the worst candidate for the event and totally unprepared. The media was there, and wouldn't you know it, the reporters zeroed in on me. I panicked when I was asked for my thoughts on the last game. I was so glad I had actually heard a little about it and could fake my way through an answer. Later, several friends told me they had seen me on TV! Bald me, on TV, talking about football—but apparently I'd pulled it off. Wonders never cease.

The game that weekend was great. Being on an actual NFL field during a game was an amazing experience, and I was thrilled that I got to be there for something that big, that loud, and that cool. A couple of months later, the American Cancer Society, which had selected me for the Crucial Catch spot, asked me to go back onto the field to accept a check on their behalf for the program. I was honored…and, of course, I was an idiot.

I was going to be down on the field holding one side of the giant check while they announced the donation to the entire crowd. The other side of the check was going to be held by a representative from the company that had donated the money. I was supposed to shake his hand when they said our names, but when I got out on the field, I was overwhelmed by the crowd, and I started waving to people in the stands and missed my cue. Suddenly, the guy holding the check with me yelled, "Hey, we are supposed to shake hands!" Meanwhile, I was smiling and waving, smiling and waving…like a fool! Even with my goofball move, it was an amazing experience to be on the field during a professional football game, and I am now a big fan of the Washington Redskins. Twice in one season I was on an actual NFL football field during real football games. Never in a million years would I have expected that would happen to me.

＝◁ ▷＝

Eventually my hair grew back, and I am now on my way to getting rid of the weight I gained during chemo. Yes, I actually gained weight during chemo. I never seem to do things the normal way— I was not sick during chemo and had a voracious appetite that I indulged. Go figure.

Maybe my perspective is different than most, but now that a couple of years have passed, I sometimes forget that I had cancer and that I spent almost a whole year battling it. However, I never thought I was going to die—that was never presented as something I needed to worry about. Cancer was more something I needed to deal with and get over. I often wonder if there was a reason for my cancer—you know, the "why me?" question. Does God have a plan for me? Was cancer part of that plan, and if so, was I supposed to have learned something? Was I supposed to have become a better person?

Most days I think there was no reason and that it boiled down to "why *not* me?" What I know for sure is that people have told me they appreciate my openness and willingness to talk about my cancer journey and that I helped them by showing an approach to cancer that went beyond the doom and gloom of the movies.

One of the biggest and best lessons I learned by going through this crap in my forties is that I can ask for help and get it. Growing up, I was taught to do things for others, but I didn't feel comfortable asking for help for myself. By battling cancer, I learned that I have a group of people close to me (both physically and spiritually) who want to help me. They helped me by showing me how amazing and supportive friendship can be and how lucky I am to have such a strong network. They helped me by going to chemo with me, by making meals for me, by taking me to lunch, by sending me gift cards, by laughing with me, by eating in public with me when I was bald or wearing a bad wig, by holding my hand, by hugging me when I cried, and by just being there for me.

This network of friends has taken decades to grow, and it may be strange to hear me say this, but I feel lucky to have gone through this in my forties. Had I been younger, my network may not have been as big, as strong, or as deep. Having been through some of life's ordeals in my twenties and thirties seemed to prepare me to survive cancer in my forties. Anyone going through a situation like cancer or other major life event needs this type of support. So, take a minute after reading this to reach out to each and every one of your friends and give them a reminder of your love through a hug, a kind note, a text, or a phone call. You need them, and they need you.

The other big lesson I learned is that as important as friends and family are in a journey like mine, believing in yourself and your strength is also important. I believe there is something deep down inside each of us that can help us climb mountains and conquer our fears. Breast cancer was a time I had to do that, and in doing it, I learned how strong I really can be when faced with a big challenge. I think I knew it was in there, but by going through this during my forties, I had enough life experiences under my belt to know I had the strength and fortitude to get through it.

And, of course, I can't end without adding the most unexpected lesson I learned—that football ain't so bad after all.

Emily Cooke is a forty-eight-year-old single, working mom with amazing breasts. Just ask—she will show you.

ASK THE AUTHORS
WHAT IS THE BEST PART ABOUT BEING FORTY?

Shannon Hembree

Embracing my inner bitch. We're halfway through our lives. We don't have to hang out with the mean girls who have grown up to be mean women. The odds are we'll all be dead in another forty years, so live it up with the lovely ladies around you who are worthy of your time and energy.

Jen McGinnis

The best part about being forty is feeling confident and (mostly) comfortable with myself. I have way less anxiety over what I do and what I don't know. I realize the kind of people I want as friends and am fine if the other ones don't think I am cool enough. I still stress about body image even though I don't want to, but I love knowing myself and feeling good about how I have chosen to live my life. I am happy.

Bree Luck

The best part about being forty is not worrying about turning forty anymore. That sounds like a small best thing, but I clawed my way up to the big four-oh. Now, safely on the other side, I can lovingly say, "Bring on the years!"

Sarah Weitzenkorn
The best part about turning forty is being able to confidently say no without an explanation.

Dionne Williams
I think the best part about being forty is that I still have my drive for life. I am going to get what I deserve, and no one is going to stop me. It's all about attitude! I live life, and life doesn't stop when you are forty. Time won't stand still, so I keep going with an even bigger passion for life than I had before.

Anne Karrick Scott Deetsch
The best part about turning forty is that you're here, and you can move on. And, you know who you are—you can have confidence in truly being yourself.

Heather Von St. James
Finally really loving who I have become, and having the desire to better myself for me, not for the sake of others. That and the ability to not give a rip what most other people think.

Barbara Fleck
The freedom that comes with knowing yourself inside and out. It makes it easier to jettison the stuff that doesn't make you happy!

Elizabeth Pendleton
That I can just be me. Turning forty gave me permission to not even try to pass for my late twenties or early thirties anymore—physically or mentally. It's a relief to be forty. I can account for all those years (and many fondly), and I like that.

Emily Cooke
The self-confidence that these decades of living have provided. Knowing that I am who I am, and I like me.

Bernadette Jasmine
The best part about turning forty is that I am finally at a point in my life where I like myself. I have forgiven myself for past mistakes. I have learned to let go and move on. All right, that might still be a work in progress, but I am grateful for what I have, and I have let go of many of the unrealistic expectations I've had about life, which has been quite liberating. And on the lighter side (literally), I have given up trying to cover up the gray hairs on my naturally brunette head with expensive salon treatments and instead have gone bottle blond. (I sense a commercial in my future...)

Vanessa Velez
For me, it's that I think I've finally learned to ignore the little things. There are things I just can't control completely, and that is okay. I think that is empowering. It was empowering for me, at least. Again, finally accepting that I will never be the perfect mother or the perfect wife was liberating. I put less pressure on myself to do everything just right.

Laura K. Bedingfield
Legitimacy. You are old enough now not to have to justify every single thing you do. Remember when your mom told you, "Because I said so, that's why"? I betcha she'd just turned forty.

Beckie Cassidy
That for whatever reason, I have the confidence to make decisions that are right for me and my family without fear of what others will think. I'm doing the best that I can for me first, and then my

husband and son, and if others don't like it, they can stick it where the sun don't shine.

Sarah Freeman Knight
The best part about being forty is that after twenty years of hair, makeup, and style mistakes, you finally have enough experience to know what looks good on you.

Jennifer Porter
Besides not having died at age thirty-nine, one of the best parts is probably not having to be bothered with knuckleheaded twenty-something-year-old "men." If you meet a knuckleheaded forty-year-old man, you can usually spot him so quickly that you save yourself time and heartache.

Rosanne Nelson
There are a million amazing things about being fortysomething. Largely, immense gratitude has replaced my twentysomething angst. Perspective has replaced thirtysomething fears. And—the most important things in my life are all under one roof.

Brooke Schmidt
Friendships. Having a clear understanding of what kinds of relationships matter, and knowing that prioritizing girlfriends is an important part of having a "whole" life.

CHAPTER 11

ON FINDING YOUR INNER WARRIOR:
HOW I LEFT A WORLD OF ABUSE AND ALCOHOLISM BEHIND AND BUILT A NEW LIFE AS THE MOTHER OF A BEAUTIFUL BOY WITH SPECIAL NEEDS

By Bernadette Jasmine

Welcome to forty. You have it all. A successful career, a shared loving and nurturing marriage with your best friend, and a beautiful home filled with healthy children. Well, not exactly...

By the time you reach forty, you expect to have it all figured out and be living the life of your dreams. That's what I thought, anyway. My thirties started out pretty good. I was living in Telluride, Colorado, the "Jewel of the San Juan Mountains." I was happily married and had a good job working in local government. My husband was a carpenter building multi-million-dollar homes for the rich and famous, and we were well on our way to success. We had a large group of close friends, and we were having a blast. We spent time skiing, dirt-bike riding, camping, hiking fourteen-thousand-foot peaks, and walking through fields of wildflowers. We loved music, especially live music, and danced a lot. Life was great. It was better than I ever could have dreamed. Little did I know that the fairy tale was about to start unraveling.

My husband and I decided to build our own home, something small to get us started, and we bought a lot in a subdivision at the end of town. This seemed like the next logical step, and I was excited to have a home of our own. We were both enamored with the idea of designing and building the house ourselves. But the novelty of that idea wore off quickly. You know the old saying: "build a house, lose a spouse." Well, that almost came true in our case. I was still working at my regular job during the day and then coming home and working evenings and weekends on the house. My husband was working on the house full time. It wasn't long before we both started to burn out. We seemed to be fighting all the time, and I noticed that my husband was drinking more and more. I think we were both too proud to give up or even take a break. It took us about six months, but we eventually finished the house and were able to move in.

The joy of being in our new home did little to repair the damage the previous six months had done to our marriage. We were still fighting, and my husband's drinking was getting worse. I thought starting a family would help things—maybe get us to settle down and refocus our direction in life. Looking back on it now, I clearly see the folly of such thinking. At the time, though, I was sure we were just stuck in a bit of a rut and that we would be able to turn things around. However, starting a family turned out to be another obstacle. I got pregnant almost immediately, but twelve weeks into the pregnancy, we were told there was no heartbeat and that we had lost our baby. I didn't become pregnant again until two years later. Things seemed to be going better this time, and when my twenty-week ultrasound came around, all I was thinking about was whether I wanted to know if I was having a boy or a girl.

But by the ultrasound technician's expression, I knew immediately that something was wrong, and my doctor came in shortly afterward and confirmed my fears. I was going to have a baby with physical deformities due to a condition known as amniotic band syndrome (ABS). ABS occurs due to a partial rupture of the amniotic sac. Fibrous bands of the amnion float in the amniotic fluid and can encircle and trap some parts of the fetus. In a large number of cases, the baby is born with clubbed feet. If a band becomes wrapped around the umbilical cord, ABS can also cause a miscarriage.

I felt like I had been sucker punched. That feeling was magnified exponentially when the doctor matter-of-factly instructed me not to go home and Google ABS and then escorted me out a back door so as not to distress the other mothers with "normal" pregnancies. That is how my journey with a son with special needs began.

The doctors assured us that ABS occurs randomly, that it's neither genetic nor caused by anything a mom did or didn't do during pregnancy. I can't begin to describe how horrible it is to feel that you can't even protect your baby inside your very own womb.

I started having contractions during week twenty-three and was put on bed rest. I had been consulting with a specialist familiar with ABS, and during my last appointment, I was rushed via ambulance to the hospital.

While in the hospital, I had several weeks to take in all the possibilities of having such a premature baby—cerebral palsy, undeveloped lungs, brain bleeds, and—the worst fear of all—that my baby might not actually survive. From what the doctors could tell, the amniotic bands were wrapped around my baby's mouth and the umbilical cord. The baby's heartbeat began to decelerate, and I was on monitors and watched around the clock. My water broke, and twenty-four hours later—at the end of my twenty-sixth week—my son, Jakob, was delivered via C-section. Weighing in at one pound, fourteen ounces, Jakob was diagnosed with chronic lung disease. His feet were turned in and up due to the clubbed feet, and the amniotic bands had taken his right index finger and more than half his right thumb and left a ring indentation on his right middle finger. The medical staff all kept congratulating me, which seemed odd at the time, because I wasn't even sure if he was going to survive the night.

We spent the next three months in the NICU at University of Colorado Hospital in Denver seven hours from my home in Telluride. I applied to move into a Ronald McDonald house but was on a waiting list for two weeks. That's when I got the first of many tiny miracles. One of the nurses who took care of me in the hospital opened her home to me. I juggled working remotely from her house and the hospital library while going to Jakob's care sessions at the NICU. At first, my physical contact with him was very limited, but eventually I was able to do kangaroo care, holding him against my bare chest, and our bonding finally started.

When Jakob left the hospital three months later, he was on supplemental oxygen constantly, and we continued to see specialists for his lungs, hand, and feet, which meant driving back to Denver for appointments. At one point, he was labeled as failure to thrive because of the altitude in Colorado. To help his lung development, Jakob and I moved in with my dad in New York for about six months. During this time, we worked with an occupational therapist, a physical therapist, a nutritionist, and a speech therapist. Jakob has undergone two hand surgeries and three foot surgeries thus far. He has also undergone serial casting and nighttime and daytime braces to help correct the clubbed feet.

While we were in New York, my husband stayed in Colorado. I had broached the subject of his coming with us, as I could surely have used the help with our son, but he refused. It was just another sign pointing to how badly our marriage had deteriorated.

After a six-month stay in New York with my dad, Jakob's lungs had developed and strengthened enough for us to return to Colorado. He still needed supplemental oxygen on occasion, and we were still dealing with the issues with his hand and feet. My focus at this point was 100 percent on our son, and thankfully things finally started to stabilize with him. My marriage, however, was a different story.

My husband had completely slipped into the depths of alcoholism. If he wasn't drunk, he was passed out somewhere. The emotional and verbal abuse became unbearable, and I spent my days walking on eggshells. I did not feel safe leaving Jakob alone with him, so I quit my job and started running a day care out of my home. Having the time with Jakob was wonderful, but money became even more of an issue. Shortly after opening my day care, my husband lost his job. His boss suspected that he was drinking on the job and couldn't afford the liability. Gulp. Now what were we going to do?

We put the house on the market, and my husband went to work for his mom in North Carolina. Jakob and I followed shortly afterward, but I knew my next course was to leave him, and I knew the only place I could go would be to family on the East Coast.

We spent the next four months living with my mother-in-law while my husband drank the days away. The final straw for me was coming out of the bedroom to find him passed out on the living-room couch with my two-year-old tapping the side of his face, saying, "Wake up, Daddy. Please wake up."

To this day, I am not exactly sure how I did it. Perhaps the stars aligned and my guardian angels circled the wagons, but I got us out of there. We headed to Connecticut to seek refuge with my sister and brother-in-law.

And that is how the decade of my forties dawned for me. I woke up in bed one morning to find myself living in my sister's home after leaving my husband of eleven years, because he had a better relationship with Jack Daniel's and Jim Beam than he did with me. Happy birthday to me.

Winding up in that situation is not an easy thing. It's the emergency exit you glance at when you're walking through a building, a door that nobody ever imagines taking. I certainly didn't. Only then I had to.

My husband's emotional and verbal abuse had begun to take its toll, and I felt like I was dying from the inside out. At some point, I figured out that you don't have to show up at the ER with a black eye or a bruise on your cheek to be abused. I had lost everything—my marriage, my home, my security, my job, and most importantly, my self-confidence and self-worth. You think to yourself that it can't get much worse, and you're right. You have hit rock bottom. I just wanted to lie back down, pull the covers over my head, and wait for the nightmare to end. But then I remembered that I hadn't lost everything. Lying in the bed next to me was my sweet little three-year-old boy. Looking at him, I knew that giving up wasn't an option. I loved him more than life itself, and he was depending on me. It is moments like this, when you are at your lowest, that you know you need to pick yourself up and do something to rise above the ashes and bring happiness and joy back into your life.

I started searching for a job, uploading résumés for hours on end. Of course, just my luck—it was the height of the recession, and countless others were desperately seeking employment right along with me. While I searched for the ever-elusive job, I was also caring for Jakob and looking for doctors to support his many needs.

Around this time, I walked through the doors of Social Services for the first time in my life and reluctantly filled out the request form for food stamps and state health insurance. Every time I went to the grocery store, I was nervous that someone I knew would end up behind me and would see me using my EBT card. But I was also very grateful for that lifeline and for the state insurance that helped with every trip to the pediatrician, pulmonologist, and orthopedic surgeon.

After more endless hours of searching and struggling, I ended up getting a job in child care as the lead teacher in the infant room at a local Montessori school. I loved the kids and was thrilled about the opportunity, but it was difficult caring for someone else's child while my own son attended preschool. The time he spent with other children was good for him, though, and being away from my ever-watchful eye helped him foster some independence and self-confidence. He was still getting sick a lot, but with each passing year, he seemed to be getting stronger, and those little illnesses didn't pose as much of a threat as they once did.

With at least one part of my life settled, I now took some time to focus on myself. I started meditating and beginning the long process of self-forgiveness. I needed to love myself again and be proud of who I was. Quieting my mind was essential to my transformation. I was also still looking for a job that would better meet my financial needs, and I eventually received a call from a recruiter asking if I would be interested in interviewing for a position with GM. I remember thinking it was too good to be true, that it had to be a scam. But it wasn't a scam, and my interview was scheduled. I hadn't been that nervous in a long time. I remember sitting on my hands before the interview to keep them from shaking in my excitement. And after the interview as I waited for the call back, it was just as bad. Would I get the job or wouldn't I? The call finally came, and I was in!

The remainder of that year, I felt that things had finally started to flow in my direction, and it seemed like I was getting my groove back. My son was growing healthier each day. I had a good job. I was able to get off the food stamps and put my son on my own insurance plan. My divorce was finalized, and I was awarded sole legal custody of my son. I began to focus on taking the next step, which was getting a place of our own, and that took the form of getting an apartment close to where I was working.

A strange thing about getting your life settled is that you begin to notice other areas of your life that are still unsettled. With everything I had accomplished, I was now becoming more aware of my own loneliness. I had very few friends locally, and juggling a career as a single mom didn't leave a lot of time for much else. I longed for companionship—for someone to cook and dance in the kitchen with. I wanted to love and be loved by someone who would respect me and love my son. But who would date someone my age—and with such a young son? My bar-hopping days were long over, and I didn't want to meet someone that way, anyway. When I was married and heard about online dating, I thought it was a bizarre and scary way to try to meet someone. I could never in a million years see myself doing something like that! That memory came back to me as I was filling out my online profile for Match.com. I still thought it was a little bizarre, but I swallowed hard and posted my profile anyway. Needless to say, my family was a little concerned. I had already come through so much and was finally back on my feet, strong and whole. They wondered why in the world I would want to throw another man into the mix. The only way I can explain it is that I'd always wanted that happy little family. I'd never wanted to get divorced or to be raising a son on my own. This was an opportunity for me to be able to share my life with someone again. But I knew it needed to be the right person.

What I found is that online dating is a lot like interviewing job candidates. You can easily weed out the less desirable prospects right off the bat.

"Hi. My name is Steve. Would you be interested in having a threesome?"

Um...NEXT!

"Hi. My name is Drew. I am not divorced yet and still living with my wife, but..."

Thank you for your interest…BUT SEE YA!

Sometimes the undesirables still get through, and you actually agree to meet them for coffee. As you sit across from the guy at Starbucks, mesmerized by his toothless grin and unibrow that appears to move of its own accord, as if something is actually living in there, you realize you need to step up your investigatory standards before you allow this to happen again. Word to the wise—when someone insists you meet them at their house for the first date, Google them. I once had a handsome emergency-room doctor send me an e-mail. We started talking, and he asked me to meet him for dinner. He was adamant that I meet him at his home first. He started texting me, and the texts became more and more risqué, which was really inappropriate at that stage in the game, considering we hadn't even met yet. I decided to do a little research on the good doctor. Thanks to the Internet, I found out that he'd had previous charges of patient molestation filed against him.

Don't call us; we'll call you.

The world of online dating can definitely be dicey, but with a little perseverance, patience, and blood work (just kidding about the last one, although it could have come in handy!), you can find some decent people out there. I was just about ready to give up on the whole thing when the right person did come along—not just someone to pass the time with, but someone who would grow to respect and love me and my son—someone I wanted to share my life with again. We have now been together for several years and recently got married.

My son, Jakob, is now nine years old. His lungs have matured and healed. He no longer needs to see a pulmonologist, and he doesn't need a nebulizer or any other preventative asthma medication. His hand is functional, and he has adapted to the anomaly very well. His latest foot surgery was successful, but we still need to consult with an orthopedic surgeon, and future surgeries are likely. He is an intelligent and well-adjusted kid, and he really is just like any other nine-year-old boy. He loves Iron Man, playing with Legos, and jumping and climbing. He also plays baseball and hockey and can skate circles around me on the ice. All in all, he has a lot of friends and is very happy.

Jakob is very much aware of his physical differences. He does ask tough questions, which always have the ability to take my breath away at first, so I have to stop and regain my composure before I answer. I try to be as honest and as loving as I can. He has asked me whether his fingers will grow back when he grows up and if his right hand will look like his other hand. I just take him on my lap, hold his hand, and tell him that this will always be his hand and that it will not change when he gets older. I tell him that his hand is beautiful but that it does look different—and that being different is okay and that everyone has differences, some visible and some not.

When someone asks him about his hand, I try to talk to him about it afterward, telling him it's okay to tell people that this is how he was born and that it doesn't hurt him, that it just looks different. I also tell him to never hide his hand and that he is beautiful in every way and should never be ashamed. I never say the words, "You can't do that because of your hand." While Jakob can be self-conscious about his hand, I also think it makes him more determined to succeed. He is fearless about trying new things, and I encourage him in this respect. I am confident he will find out on his own what he enjoys and what he is best at, just like everyone else. At age nine, some of those things include ice skating, hockey, skiing, baseball, riding dirt bikes, and drawing.

I know that a lot of women dread turning forty. I'm here to say that yes, it's a decade (like all the others) that can be filled with crazy challenge, but it can also be a time of saving yourself and reinventing yourself. Being forty is freeing. It's a time when you no longer care as much what other people think—when you long for Friday night so that you can curl up in your pajamas with a glass of wine and watch a movie and be in bed at ten instead of heading out for the night. Being forty is knowing what relationships you want in your life, fostering the ones that nourish you, and stepping away from the ones that don't. My life has vastly improved, but I still face challenges like everyone else. One of the biggest for me, particularly as the mom of a child with special needs, is not letting Jakob see my fears, worries, and anxieties and letting go of being so overprotective—just letting him be a little boy. I feel like I am doing well in that regard. For the most part, I no longer even think about Jakob's being different from other kids, and I find it such a blessing that he has adapted so well.

Since my journey began, I have learned that I am really tough—a lot stronger than I ever thought I could be. I have also learned that in order for me to be a good mom, I need to make time for myself once in a while and not feel guilty about that. I have to seek out my own interests and surround myself with people who support and encourage my endeavors. The greatest help, of course, is the unending love and support from my family.

A lot of people ask me what advice I would give to women in similar situations—those who have children with special needs. My answer is always the same: love, love, love your child, but remember that it's also important to love yourself. Self-blame and guilt do nothing to change the situation or to make you feel better—trust me, I know. You did nothing wrong; you were just blessed with a child who has different needs than most. You have to trust that you can do this. All you have to do is look into their little face, and you will find the courage you need to move forward. I found an online group for parents of children with ABS and joined their e-mail roster, which was a huge comfort, especially during those first six months. You will be amazed at how many other people are going through the exact same thing, and it's just as important to try to expose your child to other children with similar circumstances. That is what helped us, anyway.

I also tell people that sometimes you have to travel down a rough road to get where you were meant to be. Whether you are twenty, forty, sixty, eighty, or a hundred, life is bound to be full of surprises, both good and bad. I'm not sure why things happen one way or the other, but I am sure of this: you never know how strong you are until you need that strength. I have seen it in me, and I have seen it in my son. From my son in particular, I have learned so much, and I am in awe of his unfaltering spirit and determination. As I watch him skate past me at Mach speed on the ice, he will catch my gaze, smile, and proudly say, "Look, Mom! Watch me turn! I got this!" At moments like those, I know he's stronger than I ever thought possible and that he's got what it takes to be successful, no matter what life throws his way. He is going to be just fine. We both are.

⇥⊢⊣⇤

Bernadette Jasmine is a rockin' career woman who has been to the dark side and come out on top. After writing this chapter, her son, Jakob, was diagnosed with epilepsy. He continues to amaze his mom with his unflagging courage, strength, and exuberance for life, and she continues to embrace the surprises life throws at her with her happy (and slightly crazy) clan of family and friends by her side.

CHAPTER 12

ON MARRIAGE:
REDEFINING HAPPILY EVER AFTER

By Vanessa Velez

D o you remember when you found and married your Prince Charming and how full of rainbows and unicorns your relationship was back then? That's how I remember marriage in my late twenties. But now that I'm in my forties, the rainbows don't occur as often, and the unicorns have gone away. Okay, not entirely, but my vision of what it means to ride off into the sunset and live happily ever after has certainly changed. Because what exactly does living happily ever after mean when it comes to marriage?

Marriage in my late twenties was awesome. We had a little apartment. We hung out with friends. We took lots of trips. Our careers were starting to take shape. We slept in on the weekends, and on some lazy Sundays, we didn't even leave our bed. Our life was great. I got to hang out with my best friend all the time, and we could do whatever we wanted, whenever we wanted.

Then we decided we should start a family (cue ominous music). Well, *I* probably decided it was time to start a family, and my husband agreed, although I'm sure he would have welcomed a few more years of just the two of us.

We didn't realize at the time how much kids change your life. Yeah, yeah, we knew our lives would change. Everyone tells you that. Although people tend to tell you that parenthood "changes your life for the better" or that "it is the most amazing thing that will ever happen to you." And while all of that is true, there is also a darker side to parenting—the side that other parents don't tell you about because they want you to eventually become one of them, like a cult of sleep-deprived zombies so that they are not alone. Or maybe they are just afraid to admit that there is a dark side?

No one ever really talks about the pressure having kids can put on a couple—both emotionally and physically. There is a reason why sleep deprivation is called a form of torture! Having two sleep-deprived people in a house, both feeling underappreciated for their contributions, can lead to some epic fights. For example, when our son was born, he wanted to nurse *every two hours*. I did not have the good fortune of having an endless supply of breast milk, which only made a ridiculously challenging situation even more challenging. My husband came home after work one evening to find me in all of my new-mommy glory: I was still in my pajamas. I had not showered. In fact, I don't think I'd even had a chance to brush my teeth. He unwisely commented on my appearance—something to the effect that I looked like a truck had run me over. Let's just say the explosion was so spectacular that he made a very wise decision to get up with the baby in the middle of the night so that I could get some sleep.

But we survived. Our son survived. We were great. Living happily ever after.

But, as I came to realize later, our little fairy-tale life was starting to fracture. Marriage in our thirties (the decade of having young children in our house) turned out to be challenging. *Very* challenging. The year my son was born, he was my sole focus, and my husband took a backseat. At the time, I honestly just didn't see it. I figured we were both so immersed in all things baby that there were no issues. We were happy living our happily ever after. We had thriving careers. We were doing well financially. We had started a family. We were surrounded by wonderful friends. We'd just bought a house. Life was perfect. Or so I thought.

Then one day my Prince Charming told me he wasn't happy.

What the hell are you talking about? I thought. We *are* happy. Why wouldn't we be happy?

He said that he missed me, but it still wasn't sinking in.

What the hell do you mean you miss me? I railed inside. I'm right here. I haven't gone anywhere!

He calmly explained that his partner, his lover, had disappeared and had been replaced by a mom—a mom who rightfully was putting her child's needs first. But as much as he loved our son, he missed *me*.

That was really hard to hear. Had I changed that much? My first thought was that there was someone else. But he put me at ease, assuring me there was no one else. However, he was reaching out to me. He was communicating his feelings, and if I didn't take him seriously and do something to address his concerns, I could lose him to someone who would put him first.

Over the next few years, I bent over backward to make sure that both my son *and* my husband were happy. I remained focused on my son. He would always come first, but now I also made time for my husband. Date nights were instituted as a must, and we decided that we needed to get away, even if it was just overnight somewhere nearby. Those little things made a *huge* difference, but my insecurities were amplified. I would find myself thinking that he could walk away at any minute. He could ask for a divorce. I kept telling myself that I needed to make sure that he was happy *and* that our son was happy.

In that struggle, I lost myself.

My entire life became all about my husband and all about my son. I was always worried about their happiness, which meant that there was never enough time to worry about my own.

When our daughter was born, I was an emotional mess. The challenges of having a baby weren't as great, because we knew what to do and what to expect. Having the baby was the easy part. But I worried all the time. I worried that my husband would feel ignored again and that taking a backseat to not one but two children would be too much.

And then it happened. I caught him in a lie. He had told me he was meeting a friend after work, and when he came home, he told me about their night. He didn't go into a lot of detail, just telling me where they'd met up and so on. I didn't think anything of it. A few days later, a colleague told me she thought she'd seen my husband a few nights ago. She said she didn't get a chance to say hello because the place was crowded and he was on the other side of the bar. I told her that he'd mentioned that the place he went was crowded...but then she said that's not where she'd seen him. It had been somewhere else. More specifically, it had been somewhere *other* than the bar he'd told me he'd been at with his friend.

My heart stopped. He had lied. Why would he lie? It took everything I had to keep it together and not start crying. All my insecurities came rushing in at once. There was only one reason he would lie. He'd been with another woman.

My husband, of course, was traveling when I found this out. When he called that night to say good night and let me know he'd landed safely, he did all the talking for the first few minutes. Then I just asked him flat out if he was having an affair. He quickly said no, asking why I would think that. Surprisingly, at that point I was calm. Eerily calm, actually. Like the calm before a tsunami. I explained what I had learned. I didn't ask if it could be a mistake. I didn't dance around the issue. I simply asked him why he had lied.

He didn't deny it. He said that prior to meeting up with his friend, which he had told me about, he'd met up with another friend—a woman that I was not particularly fond of. His excuse was that he knew I wouldn't like it. They were meeting up to talk about a couple of work-related things, after which he went to meet up with his other friend. He said he hadn't felt like fighting about meeting up with her, so he just didn't mention it.

To say that I was hurt and angry would be an understatement of the greatest proportion, but my anger wasn't just because he'd lied. I was angry because for the last few years, I had been busting my ass to make sure that he was happy, and he'd lied to me. He shattered my trust with that lie—and my faith in the strength of our marriage. To me, it wasn't just a lie; it was a huge neon sign that nothing I had been doing mattered. All the years of insecurities, frustrations, always putting the kids and him first—of losing myself because I just didn't have any energy left—and he'd lied to me.

I didn't erupt in a spectacular explosion of screaming and yelling and threats. I was calm. (Again, eerily calm, to be exact. It scared the shit out of him, and to be honest, I think I even scared myself.) I asked if he had feelings for her. He said no, but why—if it was as innocent as he was making it out to be—had he lied? What else was he lying about?

I should note that at this point, the whole, "I didn't lie; I omitted the truth" bit got old, and it got old fast. It was like an Ally McBeal episode, where the scene she was imagining in her head would play out for the audience, because at that very moment, the scene that was playing in my mind was of me hitting him upside the head with a frying pan! I didn't do it, of course. Instead, I told him that *I* wasn't happy. I told him that I had gotten so caught up in trying to make sure *he* was happy that I'd forgotten about myself.

His response? He told me he felt like he was taking a backseat to the kids, and he missed me.

Once again, it was all about him. What about me? This is where the tsunami-type explosion happened. At that moment, I think he began to realize that he was in the wrong and how selfish he had been. And wrong—have I mentioned wrong? So very, very wrong. Getting-hit-upside-the-head-with-a-frying-pan wrong.

But in the middle of all the crying and yelling, something really great happened. We started to talk about *our* needs. I didn't know it then, but that lie was the best thing that had happened to our relationship in a long time.

I stopped crying. I stopped shaking. I wasn't angry anymore. I was just hurt. Although I felt sad, I felt good. To finally let out all the things I had been keeping bottled up—all the things I hadn't wanted to admit to myself—was such a relief. All I had been able to think about was keeping my family together, but at what cost? What if we couldn't be happy? What if we had already lost our happily ever after? What if he wasn't in love with me anymore? Or worse, what if I was tired of putting him first? What if *I* was the one who wanted out? Would I force this marriage to work just to keep our family together?

When my husband came home from his trip, we went away for the weekend. We left the kids with my parents and drove to one of our favorite B and Bs. It was the most awful car ride ever. I barely spoke the entire way. My husband tried to get a few conversations going, and I played along with one-word answers. I will admit, he almost got me when he started to tell me about a study done in the UK on beer goggles, how it's true that after consuming large amounts of alcohol, people start to look better and better. It was pretty funny, but I wasn't ready to be charmed. I think that first night he slept with one eye open (and rightfully so). He knows what to do with me when I am screaming and yelling. He has no clue what to do when I am calm and quiet.

That was a long and at times uncomfortable weekend. We were both very honest about our feelings, our frustrations, and our needs. Hearing what the other had to say was hard for each of us, but we had to do it.

In the end, we were all the better for it. We had a new appreciation and understanding of each other and our respective needs. We realized that we had to strike a balance. More importantly (and maybe most importantly), I also realized that I will never be the perfect wife or the perfect mother or the perfect employee or the perfect friend. Finally accepting that made a huge difference for me. I also promised myself that I would make more time for me.

So, what does all that have to do with being forty—or being married in your forties? On the bright side, marriage in my forties is a hell of a lot more fun than it was when I was in my thirties. (See, there *are* benefits of aging!) Sure, we still have the challenges of parenthood. My husband can still be a stubborn ass and still struggles to say the words, "I'm sorry," and I can be just as demanding and challenging as he can. But going through all the crap we did in our thirties helped us grow both as people and as partners. I think we have a deeper appreciation of who we are as individuals and what it takes to make a marriage work—well, what it takes to make *our* marriage work.

Being fortysomething has other perks as well. We have a lot more flexibility now that our careers are more established and our kids are older. We are more financially secure and able to do more things, like traveling, in ways that we just couldn't afford to when we were younger. For my fortieth birthday, my husband surprised me with a trip to Florence, Italy. It was the most romantic trip we have ever taken. We reconnected, and it was a great reminder that we still enjoy making each other laugh and that we truly do enjoy each other's company. His smile still gives me butterflies in my stomach, and every time he puts his hand on the small of my back, it still gives me chills. We don't completely forget those things when we're at home, but it's definitely harder to express those feelings when the kids want all our attention. That's why weekend getaways are crucial for us. They give us a chance to hit pause from the craziness of everyday life and just enjoy each other.

Another thing we've found is that date nights are different now. Given what we have going on in our lives, sometimes we have to *make* time—whenever and wherever we can find it. When we were younger, date nights were every night. Now they aren't always possible, so we have to get creative. Some nights we come home, catch up with the kids, and then disappear for cocktails into our study. Sometimes we let the kids in, and sometimes we shut the door. The kids often manage to find an excuse to barge in, which is fine, although one of these days, we may actually have to put a lock on the door. Just kidding...

We are also slowly turning our basement into our very own pub. All that's missing is an Irish singer. Even though we're in our forties, we can still hang out—but we can also admit that we're too old for some of the craziness of bar life, and it's nice to have an alternative in our own basement where we can get as silly and stupid as we want. Well, within reason. We do have two young and impressionable children at home. And a side note—making sure your kids are in bed when you have an at-home date night can be important. Nothing kills the moment like getting caught making out like teenagers by your twelve-year-old!

As for our happily ever after, we're still working on it with our creative date nights and our weekend getaways. When my husband first told me he was unhappy, we promised each other that we would always talk. We have kept that promise, but over the years, we learned that listening is also crucial. Talking isn't enough if your partner isn't going to listen and try to address areas of concern. Communicating isn't enough if your partner isn't going to commit to making as many decisions to love as possible.

What *is* making a decision to love? Well, it's really about picking your battles and showing appreciation whenever you can. It's about the little things we can do for each other in the craziness of everyday life to show how much we appreciate each other. With two kids and busy careers, we can't always get away to show each other how we feel, so finding ways to let each other know that we care is important.

Marriage in our forties is very different from when we were younger. Sure, there are some things we miss (like rainbows and unicorns), but we are doing our best to try to get some of them back and to discover new things to enjoy together. We've learned a lot along the way, and we will no doubt keep learning, but all in all, I wouldn't trade any of the challenges or struggles. I am living in my happily ever after.

The challenges we faced—and will continue to face—weren't in my twentysomething vision of how my marriage would unfold, but they are a part of how my happily ever after in my forties *did* unfold—kids, wrinkles, a few extra pounds, road bumps, and all.

So, here I am in our homemade Irish pub, raising a pint to all you fortysomething-year-old women out there. May you find your happily ever after—as defined by you and no one else.

Vanessa Velez is a policy consultant raising two children with the man of her dreams. She has no regrets about a life without unicorns and instead enjoys quiet evenings at home in her very own Irish pub.

CHAPTER 13

ON STRENGTH:
UNCOVERING MY INNATE POWER, BARF BY BARF AND POKE BY POKE

By Laura K. Bedingfield

When I was a child, two things could instantly throw me into a tailspin of pure, unadulterated panic: needles and vomit. Of course, neither of these things rank high on a person's wish list; however, with age (typically) comes a sense of maturity, and one learns coping mechanisms for dealing with interactions with situations that we loathe. One learns how to muscle through being uncomfortable, learn how to truly be strong.

One day I'll be brave and strong, I'd tell myself time and again, yet over and over, I would crumble into a blithering idiot whenever I crossed paths with things like booster shots or the stomach virus. I also nearly fainted when I had blood drawn from my arm for the first time in my life at age thirty-two, prior to getting married.

"Just do me a favor and don't get pregnant quickly," my doctor said to me, shaking her head as she held my trembling hand while the poor nurse drew the blood and rolled her eyes. I was weeping like a kid who'd just dropped her ice-cream cone. Oh, don't you worry, I thought to myself. Don't you worry.

Six months later, I was pregnant and back in her office, so emotionally freaked out that she asked if ours was a wanted pregnancy (which it was, of course). I sat next to her desk, face tingling and heart racing, while my doctor and my husband cracked jokes about female body parts. Their empathy for my fear was practically nonexistent. My husband had once *watched* while an orthopedic surgeon reconstructed a torn tendon in his hand.

I made it through that first pregnancy one day at a time. Instead of viewing it as a mountain to be scaled, I focused on climbing up a tiny portion of the path each day. But failing my glucose test and having to endure the three-hour one—the one that involves four separate blood draws—was a curve ball. And being RH negative meant I had to endure the RhoGAM shot…several times. As for getting the baby out of me, my main fear was not labor or the delivery. It was getting the epidural. I spent forty weeks a walking, nervous wreck.

But I walked out of the hospital nine months later feeling like Wonder Woman. In fact, the very first words I said to my husband as the doctor placed our son in my arms were, "I did it! I did it! I can't believe I did it!" The "it" in that statement wasn't so much that I'd given birth; it was that I'd finished a marathon dotted with a few weeks of typical morning sickness, seven blood draws, three RhoGAM shots, one IV, and one epidural (yes, I kept count). The baby was just the bonus. Maybe I'd finally become the brave and strong girl I'd always hoped I'd be.

Bolstered by my newfound courage (and concerned about my slowly advancing age), we hoped to quickly add to our family. Four days after our son turned one, I found out that our second baby was on the way. Nerves and anxiety got the best of me, and I found myself confiding about the new baby to a friend during a playdate between our toddlers and, as our freshly turned one-year-olds bashed trains together on the train table, breaking into tears over the fear of being pregnant again. I think I was barely four weeks pregnant.

A mere two weeks later, I began to realize that my first pregnancy, the thing that had given me the strength to think of myself as Wonder Woman, was truly just a warm-up. My fear of vomiting was about to go head-to-head against a terrible, terrible beast called hyperemesis gravidarum, or HG, a life-threatening condition that affects 1.5 to 2 percent of all pregnant women.

Ever since the Duchess of Cambridge was hospitalized for it, HG has finally gotten the attention it deserves. HG is not morning sickness. It's not even close. To say that HG is "just severe morning sickness" is like saying your kid's Little League game is the equivalent of the World Series. It's saying a nomad's sandy tent is the Burj Khalifa in Dubai. Morning sickness and HG aren't just on two different levels; they are in two separate universes.

I began vomiting when I was six weeks and three days pregnant with my son, Tucker, and did not stop until three days before I delivered him—in a spectacularly scary way—at only thirty-six weeks.

And I do mean *vomit*. Constantly. My yack counts, as I came to call them, numbered in the twenties on a daily basis.

I threw up until I had nothing left to vomit. Once you work through any residual bile in your belly (which burns your mouth and coats your throat with ulcers), you wind up with the dry heaves, which cause small fissures in your esophagus, causing you to vomit blood. I threw up until I had broken blood vessels in and around my eyes. I would wake up in the middle of the night to throw up. HG—uncontrollable, constant, extreme nausea and vomiting during pregnancy—is relentless. There is no relief. It is absolute torture.

I threw up into Ziploc bags while driving my firstborn to school. I threw up in parking lots, school restrooms, pharmacies, my OB's office, the hospital. I threw up out of car windows at red lights, into every sink in our house, in the shower. Several times I threw up until I was completely dehydrated and slipping in and out of ketosis, where your body goes into starvation mode and begins to break down fat instead of carbohydrates. Spilling ketones (+3 or over) wins you a trip to the hospital—and a visit with an IV.

At twenty-three weeks pregnant, when I had not gained a single pound, my blood pressure was 90/50, and I had thrown up twice in the examination room with the doctor standing in front of me, my OB declared that I had hyperemesis gravidarum. I lay on the examining table and cried, but I was so dehydrated that no tears even rolled down my cheeks. I was barely halfway through my pregnancy; the thought of enduring another twenty weeks of agony nearly broke me.

I learned the HG mantra of "easy down, easy up," which means that since every single thing you swallow will revisit you within the hour, you want to do all you can to make the experience as tolerable as possible. I threw up Gatorade that still had ice chunks in it (an interesting experience, by the way, especially if your throat is coated with ulcers). Anything with carbonation hurt like a mother, but Chick-fil-A sweet tea was easy. Toast? Not so delightful; it is insanely sharp and pointy. Rice comes out your nose.

When I reached twenty-eight weeks and still had not gained a pound, a Matria Healthcare nurse brought a Zofran pump to my house. The machine sat in my fridge, its needles—*needles, I say!*—and catheters scaring the bejesus out of me. I cut a deal with her instead: we maxed out my oral Zofran dosage, and if I threw up more than four times a day, I had to call her, because it was mandatory to start the pump. My husband set his alarm and woke me up nightly to make sure I got the midnight dosage of the little dissolvable pill that cost—at that time—thirty-two dollars a pop. I was taking four a day.

I wound up not being honest with the Matria nurse, clearly the low point of the entire torturous ordeal. I was lucky to only have thrown up four times by high noon. Thankfully, about the time the Matria nurse came into my life, I'd connected with other women suffering through HG on the lifesaving hyperemesis-awareness board on the Internet. I don't know how I could have made it without them. They were the toughest group of people I'd ever seen.

They warned me about the fine layer of fuzz that would grow all over my body, a mammalian defense mechanism to try to keep a malnourished body warm. They assured me that my fingernails would likely grow back even though they'd split and peeled off. They helped me find ways to avoid my triggers (certain random things that can throw you over a cliff so fast that you find yourself in the ER by sundown). They taught me things I'd never have figured out—for instance, that Pepsodent Sensitive toothpaste is the least flavored toothpaste out there, that unscented Aveeno products really are completely unscented (smells are a huge trigger for most HGers), and that deodorant doesn't really matter because it can't cover the stench of the ketones you're spilling.

They explained why bright lights and moving through shadows could crumble me in an instant. They understood why I had beach buckets in every room; they knew I wasn't kidding when I said I had to crawl from room to room in my house. These women saved me.

They taught me that I was not alone and that I was not going crazy—nor was I a wimp. They taught me that my baby was going to be one tough guy because he was enduring all this—a limited food and nutrient supply; a dehydrated, fatigued, and malnourished mother; and a constant onslaught of medicines—during the most critical stage of his life, while he was in utero. They taught me to trust that the HG would go away once I delivered my baby. They taught me that I *was* strong—stronger, and braver, and more tenacious than I'd ever imagined.

So, I set my sights on February 1 (both my due date and our wedding anniversary), and for the first time in my life, I literally marked days off the calendar as they passed.

When the calendar had barely flipped into January, I had a huge contraction and then felt a pop. I immediately assumed my water had broken.

But it wasn't my water. I was hemorrhaging.

We raced to the hospital with my son in the backseat shouting, "Go, Daddy! Go!" I tried to talk to my doctor on the phone to explain what I was feeling but had to pass it off to my husband because I could feel the blood surging with every heartbeat. By the time we reached the ER, I couldn't walk. Blood was everywhere, literally everywhere—soaked through my clothes, in puddles on the seat of the car, even as a print on the window where I'd put my hand in hopes of alerting oncoming cars as we ran red lights.

I was rushed up to a labor and delivery room packed to the gills with medical personnel. One nurse started an IV while another drew blood—all while my OB took a peek under the hood to see what was going on. My husband stood ashen in the corner, holding our toddler in his arms.

"This is a lot of blood," the doctor said, voicing my concern entirely. "We need to take the baby."

They began to prep me for surgery while my husband called family members and passed my son off to my aunt, whom we'd called to fetch him; she had almost beaten us to the hospital. I barely got to kiss the top of my son's curly head before the gurney was rolling down the hall to the operating room. I'd had such great plans for how we were going to spend the last month of his being an only child. Now I realized that not only were these the last few moments of our being a family of three, he'd not even eaten his supper yet.

A nurse helped me up onto the operating table and warned me not to look backward. I assumed this was so I wouldn't see the anesthesiologist and his epidural kit. Later I learned it was so I wouldn't see the neonatal crash team setting up all their machines and equipment in anticipation of my son's birth.

My husband wasn't allowed in the operating room just yet, so I held a stranger's hands while they placed the epidural. Time was of the essence, and the anesthesiologist told me we couldn't wait for the novocaine to set in, so I needed to take a deep breath and hang on. For the record, an epidural is *screwed* into your back, not just jabbed.

While all that was happening, I was still hemorrhaging. They laid me down on the table and pulled my arms out to the sides— landing me in a position horribly similar to crucifixion. I was light-headed and told the doctor I was going to throw up. I also announced to the entire operating room that I was dying.

I honestly believed that, too. Never have I ever been so scared.

One hour and nineteen minutes after we set foot inside the hospital, we became a family of four. At some point, they'd allowed my husband into the operating room. He stood in the distance, brandishing a borrowed camera and being warned by the doctors to NOT TOUCH ANYTHING. I have no recollection whatsoever of the photos he took, no memory of their showing my baby to me for the first time, no memory of their having to knock me out completely because the epidural was taking too long to work, no memory of their working another forty-five minutes after the birth to get the bleeding to stop. I was a passive participant in a miracle.

I'd wound up having a placental abruption. Luckily I had made it to thirty-six weeks in my pregnancy, and because of the HG, my baby was impressively resilient. He had fought for every single nutrient he could get for thirty-six weeks; this wild and crazy entry into the world was just the cherry on top, so to speak. My OB's report the next day was sobering: twenty years ago, we'd have lost the baby. Fifty years ago, we'd have lost both of us. Abruptions of 25 percent or more typically result in serious complications for the infant; thankfully, mine was only between 10 and 15 percent.

I left the hospital four days later decidedly *not* feeling like Wonder Woman. In addition to having undergone major surgery and having a premature newborn who needed to nurse every two hours, I also had a very confused nineteen-month-old who'd just been bumped from his nursery into his big-boy room less than a week before. I was too tired to play trains with him. I was too sore to play marching band with him. I howled at him if he was ever too loud and woke the (rarely sleeping) baby. I was still quite malnourished and had no taste for anything. The friend to whom I'd divulged the secret of my pregnancy just eight months earlier called one morning to tell me her husband had taken a job in Charlotte and that they were moving. She had been with me through the entire mess of a pregnancy, and her family's impending relocation broke my heart.

I spent the cold and dreary month of January in a fog. I cried (a lot). I slept (very little). I questioned everything I'd ever done and every choice I'd ever made and tried to gauge how it had affected my life's trajectory. I cried every single night as I read the book *Bounce* to my older son, a book that is definitely *not* a sad book. I cried as my younger son cried, his immature tummy hurting him so badly that he'd turn beet red and hold his breath before wailing and squirming until he'd break free of his swaddling. I cried as I nursed him in the middle of the night, convinced everyone else in the entire world was asleep but me (and my baby). I cried when the mailman delivered a package to us. I cried when the Genesis song "Follow You, Follow Me" came on the radio. An awful lot of crying was going on. It was not pretty.

But eventually, things began to turn around. The big brother started to accept that this little, screeching creature was sticking around. My baby started sleeping three-hour stretches, and then four-hour stretches—and then finally five-hour stretches (at least every few weeks). We figured out how to help him with his tummy issues. I learned how to build train tracks and play a recorder while also holding a baby. I was no longer vomiting multiple times a day.

My vigor began to come back. I gained strength—physically, mentally, and emotionally.

Then one morning as the sun was coming up, I was in the nursery, rocking and patting and humming and *begging* the baby to go back to sleep. My tiny blue-eyed son locked eyes with me and smiled for the very first time.

He had a huge, adorable, perfect dimple.

I knew then that things were going to be okay. Like Lynda Carter, who spun around and around and around during her metamorphosis from Diana Prince to superheroine, the massive, almost year-long spin cycle I'd just been through had had a purpose. I *was* brave; I *was* tough; I *was* strong. I *was* Wonder Woman. I'd made it through a crazy pregnancy, a crazy delivery, and a crazy postpartum period. But I had not quit—not once. I had muscled through it all, fighting back fear, uncertainty, and panic on a daily—sometimes hourly—basis.

If you'd told the ten-year-old me that I'd one day view needle pokes as simply a minor annoyance, that ten-year-old—who had just bloodied a doctor's lip from wrestling with him as he administered a tetanus shot—would have thought you were insane. If you'd told the twenty-year-old me that I would have to endure twenty-seven weeks and four days of nonstop vomiting, I would have reminded you that I was still traumatized from being barfed on by a friend in a car when we were three.

While I'm not exactly sure where my fortitude and courage came from, I can say that I'm very glad to have it along with me for the ride. Even though it took close to forty years to pull that strength up from my core, tendril by tendril, I'll take it. The hidden, inner strength of women is what keeps the world spinning. We are powerful without even knowing it, and we become even more powerful once we realize this innate tenacity.

Friedrich Nietzsche once wrote, "That which does not kill us makes us stronger." He was right. In the end, I was stronger than

I'd ever realized. I know now that I always *was* Wonder Woman, even though I didn't always see it.

><+ +>

Laura K. Bedingfield maintains her strength by writing, practicing yoga, scoring baseball games for her sons, driving a mean carpool, and dominating during family game night. She stockpiled her leftover Zofran and guards these pills like the pellets of gold they are. Nineteen months after her HG pregnancy, she rolled the dice and got pregnant again, a pregnancy during which she hurled only three times. Nine months later, her third son arrived via VBAC. (And sorry, Daddy, for busting your lip over that tetanus shot so long ago...)

CHAPTER 14

ON BALANCING A CAREER AND KIDS:
FINDING PERFECTION IN NOT BEING PERFECT

By Beckie Cassidy

It was around noon on a Wednesday, and I was at home, simultaneously folding laundry and waiting for some guys to drop off wood that we had purchased for a new floor in our basement. I hadn't taken the day off from work like I should have; I had snuck home at lunchtime, because apparently wood can only be dropped off smack in the middle of the day, smack in the middle of the week. Like any normal human being, I didn't want to burn a vacation day on what would essentially be a ten-minute visit. I figured that in between the e-mails I was answering to make it *look* like I was still at work, I could fold a load of laundry and still take calls from my boss compliments of my cell phone, which I was carrying in my pocket.

In the middle of doing all this, I was thinking of how to answer the question, "How does a woman in her forties with a family and a full-time job balance it all?" That's when it occurred to me: This isn't balance; this is bullshit. I'm literally doing five things at once.

How can I possibly write about balancing work, family, and life in general when all I'm really doing is multitasking—something I have enough self-awareness to know I stink at?

It was around this time that my parents paid us a visit. They turned on the TV to the sounds and sights of one of the many Viagra / Cialis / white-male-problem-drug commercials warning us viewers that if our man suffers from an erection for four hours or more, he needs to seek medical help immediately.

"I'm so glad I don't have to raise kids today," said my dad. When I looked at him a bit strangely, he followed up with "I can't imagine having to explain that to a child! The worst thing on TV when you three were kids was *Friends!*"

His comments got me thinking about how parenting has changed over the past few decades, and it made me stop and wonder how our moms and grandmas had found balance in their own lives—or if that was something they worried about at all.

My mom was a stay-at-home mom until I was about ten years old. The house was always in tip-top shape, laundry was done, dinners were cooked at home, and the yard was perfect. Although in retrospect, I chalk a lot of that up to OCD versus life balance. Around the age of nine or so, I remember waiting in the car with my younger brother and sister while my mom ran in to a greeting-card store to get a card for some occasion or other. (That was before the days of "free-range parenting," and the risk of arrest was *much* lower.) When she came out, not only did she have the greeting card but, she gasped and told us, "I think I just got a job!" She looked positively giddy, and while that job working a cash register at a greeting-card store didn't last long, it did whet her appetite for outside-the-house activities. Soon after that, she decided to go back to school for her master's degree in teaching, which then led to a job teaching in an elementary school.

As with most (if not all) moms who go back to work, she found that instead of her responsibilities shifting to the rest of us, they only increased. She was still the main person in charge of laundry, cooking, grocery shopping, and so on. One night, my mom was out at something or other, and my dad came to me to ask what was for dinner. Being the late-eighties feminist that I was, I said, "I don't know—what are you making?" And then I caved and made dinner for the family anyway. 'Cause it just wasn't his job.

I suppose it was around this time that the bar started being raised for women everywhere. Sometime in the late 1990s, I was at a family Thanksgiving, and my uncle, who was about sixty at the time, commented about how parents were now expected to go to every sporting event their child has.

"If my dad showed up to one of my baseball games," he reflected, "my first thought was 'Uh-oh, I'm in trouble. *Now* what did I do?'" Because in the 1960s, the only reason his father would go to one of his games would be to pull him out of the game for some unknown (but definitely very bad) reason.

Fast-forward fifty years. Today's helicopter-parenting phenomenon has upped the performance bar so much that if my uncle were playing baseball today, he would be doing so after a day of receiving a top-notch private-school education, and he would be on the fast-track to the major leagues—either that or Harvard. His raging success would be attributed to his innate superhuman talent, inherited from his parents' superior DNA. His parents—having attended his every practice and every game and having hired a private pitching coach on his one or two off days—would be lauded for their unwavering dedication. All this would be applauded but also expected, because for parents to do any less today is considered practically neglect.

Here is the part that baffles me the most. While many of us would describe the aforementioned scenario as craziness, we then turn around and up the bar even further in the name of good parenting.

"You buy cleaning supplies from the grocery store? I have a book for you—it tells you how to make all your cleaning supplies using nontoxic chemicals. Your kids will be healthier, and you'll save tons of cash!"

"You don't compost? We have a box of worms in our living room and a composting container in our kitchen."

"Goldfish? My kids eat black beans as finger food."

Sadly, I have been on the receiving end of all the above conversations. And let's not forget HGTV and the Food Network (and mothers-in-law) telling us how to be ready to entertain at a moment's notice. As if that's not enough, we're supposed to do all this while staying mom-magazine thin, keeping our partners happy in the sack, and maintaining a full-time job.

Today, I find myself performing many of the same tasks my mother did, to the horror of my inner feminist, but I'm a pleaser by nature. One of the best compliments I ever received was when my son was about a year old and I was working full time. My aunt said to me, "Wow, you really *are* superwoman!" Well, of course I am! My mom was superwoman, so why shouldn't I be? But then come the moments when I don't feel that way at all.

I am aware of the need for work-life balance, and I am making some sort of effort to achieve it, but every now and then I find myself in a state of burnout, where I'm so tired from being everything to everyone that I become a cranky pain in the ass—clearly failing in my mission to achieve "balance."

Recognizing that I may need some help in this area, I looked to the "experts" on how to achieve this elusive state of balance and peace while also getting everything done each day. My colleague has a poster of Rosie the Riveter in her office. I always wondered how Rosie was able to go to work in a factory while her partner was off fighting for our country. I don't know what her whole story is, whether she had kids—and if so, how she balanced it all. Given that she is mostly government propaganda, I doubt she did.

Next on my list of experts was Gloria Steinem, who famously said that she has never heard a man ask for advice on how to combine marriage and a career. So I wondered how she managed to raise kids and still have the career she did. I wondered that until I heard her say that she has always worked in a freelance capacity. She's never actually had a job in the "conventional sense." So, she's out as my role model, too.

Finally, I've tried to *Lean In* with Sheryl Sandberg, but given my lack of millions, I don't have an army of nannies and people around me to help with the laundry and everything else. So, she's off my list.

Then a funny thing happened. I turned forty and stopped caring about finding balance—or at least about what others think of me. This summer I had the "audacity" to leave a week-long family reunion a day early so that I could have a day to transition between "vacation" and work. My dad didn't talk to me for three weeks. And you know what? I didn't apologize. His opinion of my job as daughter suddenly didn't matter. I not only wanted that day, I *needed* that day. I needed it to do laundry, to catch up on sleep, and to do the thousands of other things that needed to get done before I returned to work. That was the day I found some balance in my life.

As a direct result of turning forty, I have found that within me lies the strength to say no—whether it's to attending each and every work event or to getting a PhD while I'm raising a child and working full time. For me, it comes down to letting some things go and to being okay with that. *To not being perfect.*

These days, my son has karate three times a week, and we get home at about seven thirty in the evening. On these nights, he gets chicken nuggets for dinner, because you know what? He will survive, despite his protests. I'm not a perfect mom, *and I'm okay with that.* I'm also okay with the twenty pounds I gained since I started my last job. Sure, I'll keep trying to lose it, but it certainly isn't defining who I am the way it would have even two years ago. I'm not a model. I never have been. I'm finally okay with that (sort of). And if it's true that your brain really does get stronger when you use it, then at least part of me is in fighting shape, and that is something I really am okay with, because you need all the brainpower you can get when you're trying to make it work as a working mom.

The other thing I've learned to do in my quest for balance is to *ask for help*. On any given day, I will have to prioritize work projects and meetings with my son's school projects and activities. This is especially challenging given that we are a one-car family. While I try to be good and take the somewhat reasonably priced Metro to and from work, Uber has started to show up on my credit-card statement more and more. Here is my biggest confession: I hire a cleaning service to come in twice a month to clean my house (*gasp!*). For several years I wouldn't admit this to anyone, particularly my mother (see above re: OCD), but now that I'm forty, I'm okay with asking for help, even if it means someone else has to see my mess.

My life may not be the having-it-all balance or the doing-it-all balance I imagined it would be when I was younger, but it is the right balance right now. Having experienced firsthand how hard it is to find that perfectly imperfect balance, I can't help but think that my aunt was right. I *am* superwoman. Any woman who has made it to forty and experienced all that that road entails is. We may not wear a red cape and a blue bodysuit (although wouldn't *that* be quite a sight!), but we are still out there averting disasters and swooping in with solutions day in and day out. They may not be the perfect solutions, and some days are definitely better than others (bring on the Kendall Jackson), but all in all, when you lean back and let your imperfect self enjoy it, it's a great ride.

⚔

Beckie Cassidy is a full-time working mom who is finding balance amid the goldfish (crackers and otherwise), karate lessons, and doggie day care. After spending twenty years trying to figure out what she wanted to be when she grew up, she gave up and now spends her days telling college students what they should be when they grow up.

CHAPTER 15

ON HOW IT'S NEVER TOO LATE TO FACE YOUR FEARS:
EVEN IF IT REQUIRES ALCOHOL, PILLS, OR PRAYER

By Sarah Freeman Knight

A lot of people are afraid of flying. They say they can only fly with alcohol, pills, or prayer. Then there is a smaller group of people whose fear so overwhelms them that they can't fly at all. These are the people who choose to take a train or bus across the country instead of a plane, who turn down jobs that involve travel, and who make their world smaller so that it comfortably fits within an acceptable driving radius. I was one of those people, and I had done all of those things to avoid flying.

By the time I turned forty, I hadn't flown in seventeen years, positive that setting foot on a plane would mean certain death. I had missed my sister's wedding, turned down a free trip to Europe, given up my dream job, and wasted countless hours traveling thousands of miles by car, bus, and train to avoid flying on an airplane. It was inconvenient, limiting, and sad, but I didn't care, because I was still alive. I took this as proof that I was right.

So, when I flew across the country with my husband and two daughters at the age of forty, I was taking a giant leap of faith.

Six months earlier, I was reading a magazine when I saw an ad in big, bold letters asking ARE YOU AFRAID OF FLYING? The local university was seeking participants in a virtual-reality experiment about overcoming flying phobias. I figured it was a great opportunity to get free therapy and maybe even overcome my fear.

Over the years, I had wasted a lot of money telling various therapists about my fear, only to have them explain that it was the result of being rejected by my mother and sent to live overseas with my father when I was in high school. The plane was supposed to represent all the fear and insecurity that was a part of my life at that time. Whether or not that was true, I found that focusing on the root cause of my fear was completely unhelpful, and my fear only grew over time. At this point, I wanted a practical and cheap fix, and the ad met all my requirements.

I made a phone call and immediately got accepted into the treatment program. The woman could barely hide her delight when I told her that I hadn't been able to fly for seventeen years. I would be the perfect test case.

It turns out that virtual reality—at least in this situation—was not as advanced as I had hoped. I thought it would be like in a movie. I would put a helmet on and suddenly be in a world that looks exactly the same as the real world, but even better.

It was not like that at all. For six months, I walked into a dingy office with worn carpeting, sat in a pleather chair, and put on goggles and headphones. Inside my goggles, the graphics of the airport and the airplane looked like a cartoon made in the 1950s. The pilot speaking into my ears kept repeating himself and giving inaccurate information. He would tell us that we would have clear skies, but we would hit a thunderstorm *every single time.* What was wrong with this pilot that he couldn't even read the weather reports correctly? How was I supposed to trust him with my fake life in this fake simulation if he couldn't even tell clear skies from sure disaster?

On the other hand, the pleather chair did shake, and it shook harder and harder with every lightning strike. It was hardly as scary as being on a real airplane and experiencing real turbulence, but it was scary enough for me.

The researcher was a very perky and positive young woman who just *knew* I could do it. I was less sure. She cheered for me throughout the six-month program, and we became sort-of friends—except for the part where I had to leave the second my time was up.

In addition to having to log an hour of virtual-reality flying each week in the office, I also had to do homework and field trips. I was required to read books written by pilots on a variety of subjects, and I had to learn the basics of aerodynamics, watch a children's video for first-time fliers, and practice muscle relaxation and slow breathing. I even took a field trip to the airport.

The key to overcoming a phobia, as explained to me by my researcher, is gradual exposure. She said that flying without gradual preparation—as I had forced myself to do several times after my phobia first began at fifteen until I completely stopped flying at twenty-three—would result in panic attacks and strengthen the phobia.

I told her time and time again that my fear was bigger than other people's fear (it is), to which she replied that everyone thinks this (I'm sure they don't). I told her that I had lived for seventeen years with nightmares almost every night about being on a plane. I told her that when I woke up in a panic from these nightmares, I experienced an overwhelming sense of relief that I was still in my bed. I explained that I couldn't overstate how *big* my fear was. I truly believed I would die. I couldn't even hear an airplane fly overhead without my heart racing. She just nodded her head and told me that everything I said was exactly what everyone else who was afraid to fly said.

The thing about facing a fear in your forties is that it's had the chance to get really big. That's the bad part. The good part is that you have more perspective. You realize that this is your only life and that time is running out to make your dreams come true. I have a dream of one day traveling the world, for example. I long to go to Europe, eat in Parisian cafés, see castles, and roam the Italian countryside. None of those dreams pair well with a crippling fear of flying.

Aside from my elusive dream of traveling the world (which requires not only an ability to fly but also scads of money, which is in short supply with two kids, two dogs, two cars, and a mortgage), I had two daughters who looked to me to set a good example. Being a mother made my fear infinitely bigger. What if I really did die in a plane crash, leaving my girls motherless? Even worse, what if they were with me, and my decision to take them on a plane led to their deaths? The overwhelming and crushing horror of those thoughts literally took my breath away. I couldn't let my thoughts go there if I was ever going to get on a plane.

While being a mom made getting on a plane infinitely more terrifying, it also made overcoming my fear infinitely more important. I knew that if ever I wanted to have credibility about facing fears with my kids, and if ever I was going to teach them how to overcome *their* fears, I would have to do it. It was a matter of practicality on many levels. How could I tell my daughter that she had to face her fear of werewolves and sleep alone in her bed when I couldn't face my own fear?

The airplane was my werewolf.

Sure, it seems silly. Werewolves aren't real, and people fly every day. But I come from a long line of family members who struggle with anxiety and other issues. I live in a world where regular fears have grown into something more. The difference I was finding at forty is that I had the perspective to see that the things I feared— even those things I had feared the most—were not the things that happened. Sure, scary things do happen, and I had not lost sight of that (believe me!), but the things that happened in my life aren't the ones I feared and expected. This perspective was a positive influence on my life in so many ways, but it was also a punch in the gut, because the realization came with that perspective that out of fear, I had wasted so much time and energy and made my life so small. Even more than that, I had done so out of fear of things that never happened.

For me, flying meant facing my fear. It also meant accepting the unknown and learning to trust. All these seemed like insurmountable obstacles to me, but watching my daughters begin to worry and begin to avoid things they wanted to do because they were afraid made me realize that I had no choice.

I had to get on the damned plane.

I bought the plane tickets three months into the program. I knew that if I didn't force my own hand, I would never do it.

It took me at least twenty visits to the Delta website before I was able to solemnly type our names and ages into the passenger list—the passenger list I knew they would refer to if our plane crashed in a fiery explosion. Or if we were taken hostage. Or if we were lost at sea. The possibilities were endless.

It took many more visits before I was able to click the purchase button, and when I did it, I felt sick. The plan was to fly across the country to Portland to visit my brother and his family. He had always flown out to see us, and it would be the first time I had ever visited him. The flight was five hours long from coast to coast. I chose nonstop, because I wasn't sure I would be able to get back on the plane once it landed. It was a good call.

Another good call was talking to my doctor and getting a prescription for anxiety medication prior to the flight. Virtual-reality training is good and all, but so is knowing your limits, and I was pretty sure I was about to surpass all of mine. I had researched the benefits of heavy drinking versus anxiety medication (you have to give me props for my commitment, at least) and decided that the medication looked more promising. I had to start taking it a week before the flight because I couldn't sleep.

The scariest steps I have ever taken are the steps I took that day leading from the rickety, metal gangplank onto that giant, freakish airplane—that stupid werewolf of the sky. I fought the urge to turn and run back into the safety of the airport. My children were pushing forward, excited to find their seats and go on their first plane ride, so I followed them, numb and sick, trying to remember everything I had learned in my program.

I remembered to breathe. It was the stupidest advice ever, but my therapist felt it was important. Apparently not breathing is a bad thing. I remembered to talk back to the scary voice in my head and answer all its warnings about the plane crashing with the statistics on airline safety that my therapist made me memorize. I looked around at all the bored people on the airplane who did not think we were going to die and remembered to take my cues from the reactions of normal people, since I couldn't trust my own. And...I thought about the pilots and their extensive training—and their will to live and return home safely to their own families.

I am safe right now, I told myself over and over, only to have the voice in my head shriek, "We are going to crash!" Thankfully, I remembered never to say this out loud.

Instead, I sucked in another breath and reminded myself that we hadn't even taken off yet.

My hands were shaking so badly as I sat in my seat waiting to take off that I had to force them to work so I could put on my seat belt. My kids were talking, but I couldn't focus on their words. They were having a great time, busy adjusting their new neck pillows and getting out their coloring books and plane snacks. As planned in advance, my husband was in charge of entertaining them so I could use all my energy and effort to breathe and not start screaming.

I took a second Valium. The plane backed up, turned, and then began bumping along forward. We sped up, and the noise rumbling around us became so loud it was deafening.

WE WERE IN THE AIR!

I squeezed my eyes shut and held my armrests in a death grip as we rose up from the ground.

For the next five hours, I continued to focus on my breathing. I reminded myself to relax my clenched fists. I visualized relaxing scenes. I reminded myself of the statistics. I took more Valium. Each bump sucked my newfound courage out of me, and I had to remind myself that those were a normal part of air travel. Just like a bump in the road. We were safe.

I didn't really believe it, though.

If the anxiety medication I took on the flight (a dose way higher than what was recommended...which I *don't* recommend) helped at all, I don't know, because my anxiety level was so high and so overwhelming that I couldn't imagine being more afraid. I am fairly confident that without it, however, I would have been the crazy person that other passengers tackle midflight and pin to the ground until the air marshal can put them in plastic handcuffs.

But I got through it. It was a lesson like the others I had learned during my forty years: life is scary, and terrible things happen. The only way to deal with it is to trust and to live the fullest life. I want to teach this to my children. I want to give them a world full of possibility, and someday, before I die, I want to get to Europe.

When our plane landed (miraculously), the feeling of touching the ground was amazing. The sense of relief was so total that I had to use all my strength to stop myself from pushing everyone aside and racing off the plane.

That feeling of relief turned to triumph and joy when I saw my brother and sister-in-law standing in the airport holding balloons and flowers for me (yes me, the grown adult, not my two children, as you might suppose).

At that point, my breathing and heartbeat slowed enough for me to feel the effects of the several Valiums, and things got hazy. My husband had to help guide me to the car.

>—‹‖›—

Despite the energy and fear it took to get there, we had an awesome week in Portland. Unfortunately, my fear didn't just go away in one magic trip. Dragons aren't slain with one slice of the sword—at least not a dragon this big. But I did cut my dragon down to a smaller size, and I was able to get back on the plane to go home.

The return flight was still terrifying, and I still felt like I was about to die the entire time, but it was slightly less terrifying. I was able to look out the window for a moment and watch the sun set from up high. And for just one moment, I thought the pink color streaking across the sky was beautiful, something I would have never seen from the ground. When we landed, the flight attendant said she was so impressed with how well behaved the children were (little did she know that *I* was the one she'd had to worry about) that we could go meet the pilot and sit in his chair.

With shaking hands, I snapped a picture of my two girls in the cockpit seats. They were both wearing pilot hats and beaming with their hands on the wheel.

That picture is now framed in my living room, and every time I look at it, I think of our trip together. It gives me hope that my girls' lives will always be bigger because of their courage, and it fills me with hope that mine will be too. I wish it hadn't taken me until I was forty to face my fear, but I'm thankful that I did face it.

The amazing thing about facing one fear is that it gives you more faith in yourself and in your ability to take on other challenges. You start making small daily choices that slowly expand your experiences and your life. Now I join my kids on amusement park rides instead of avoiding them. I can climb a tall mountain and remember to breathe at the top and see the beauty of the view instead of feeling only the fear of the height. I am able to look forward to the future with anticipation of all that is to come instead of only fear.

Even though I don't *want* to fly again, now I know that I *can* fly again. And the difference between being able to do something versus not being able to do something is the biggest difference in the world. I'm still hoping to make it to Europe.

Sarah Freeman Knight is a professional writer living in Atlanta. She is married to a very patient husband, who did not get enough credit for his role in this story, and is the mother of two amazing and courageous girls. She is looking forward to flying to Europe soon…unless she finds an awesome deal on the QE2 and can go by boat instead.

CHAPTER 16

ON SPIRITUALITY:
HOW A PREACHER'S DAUGHTER REDISCOVERED AND REDEFINED FAITH

By Jennifer Porter

"God doesn't care. If He does, then why is He letting this happen to me?"

I actually heard myself say this phrase aloud one morning. I was thirty-nine years old, and life had been a surprising disappointment in every way possible.

So many people have said this or something similar so many times that it's hardly noteworthy. After all, life in general is full of indignities and challenges. These range from life-robbing evil acts, like terrorism, war, and violent crime, to less catastrophic events, like losing out on that promotion, having to deal with unpleasant people, and even putting up with petty annoyances such as being cut off in traffic.

Those are just some of the human-caused maladies. Tragic accidents, weather-gone-wild events like tsunamis, hurricanes, and tornadoes (you know, "acts of God") when added to the picture have caused many people to believe God doesn't exist. Or they argue that if He does exist He certainly isn't actually running any-thing, and He doesn't care enough to do more than judge, shrug, or maybe sigh at His creation.

But my uttering the words "God doesn't care" had special sig-nificance, because I am the daughter of a Pentecostal preacher. (Think fire, brimstone, theatrical preaching, and loud, invigorat-ing music.) I had been a believer almost from the womb.

I ate, slept, and breathed religion. It defined who I was inside and out. My family's life revolved around the church and church activities, so between Sunday school, two Sunday services, mid-week Bible study, choir practice, and other assorted activities, most of my waking hours were absorbed by church.

Sundays began early with a big breakfast for eight—there were six of us kids—but if we were running late, we made do with ce-real. We would head out to Sunday school, which offered child-friendly lessons about well-known Bible characters and at least one off-tune but earnest song wrung through the children's squeaky and tender voices. Everyone was impeccably dressed in our tra-ditional "Sunday best," so the boys often fidgeted because of stiff collars and fake neckties while the girls smoothed their tights and fancy dresses that usually had tulle or lace slips sewn under the skirts.

The church buildings were small—some had been storefronts. Even so, the adults dressed totally to the nines. Every self-respect-ing Pentecostal woman wore dress shoes with a matching hand-bag and stylish hat that fit her budget. Skirts had to fall below the knees, or congregants could use a lap cloth to maintain decency. The men wore business suits, or at least blazers and ties, in all weather: hot, cold, rainy, or snowy.

The main service came after Sunday school, followed by a break when everyone went home for dinner. Most people returned for the Sunday evening service. If it was a "big Sunday," another congregation would come visit, or ours would go to visit them, and nothing got done unless it was accompanied by singing. Even if the organist or pianist was late—or didn't show at all—the music still flowed. Someone who'd had a few lessons would move to the bench, or another instrument like the guitar would lead. Musical talent flows through my family, so we were always in the choir or chorales, and my three brothers became the church's rhythm section, playing guitar, drums, and bass.

I thought the singing was routine until I grew up and attended other denominations of churches. Although we occasionally sang standard hymns, the spirituals, choruses, and gospel numbers were the highlights of our services. From the elderly members who could belt out tunes a cappella to the younger members who sang modern gospel numbers each week, it was almost like a full-fledged concert. The point of each service was to feel "the Spirit," which wasn't difficult in the highly charged atmosphere.

This was a weekly routine. Plus, if my dad felt we'd missed a service or two during the week, we might kick off the weekend by having a Friday-night Bible study at home.

I lived in a black, lower-middle-class neighborhood in Connecticut, but at the age of ten, I escaped the shoddy school system by testing into a magnet program and then going to an overwhelmingly white private school. After graduating, I attended a top-ranked university, obtained a master's degree, and gained some semblance of middle-class life. This was a major accomplishment in my family, since my father had come to the United States from Jamaica as a migrant farm worker and my mother had grown up in public housing, held a high school diploma, and had trained as a seamstress.

Few people in my Connecticut prep school knew that my childhood experience included church attendance several days a week complete with long, "high-energy" worship services and other hallmarks of Pentecostalism. This was the beginning of my penchant for living in two worlds. I commuted by city bus from my low-income neighborhood and alighted clear across town in the suburbs, where my days were spent with affluent, preppy classmates. This was when I learned that families actually traveled for vacations—with beaches, not churches, as their final destinations.

When I entered college, I left Pentecostalism behind and acted decidedly un-Pentecostal. Engaging in typical college life became routine, but I didn't abandon religion entirely. At no point did I doubt God's existence, and I'd argue vehemently with classmates who were atheists. After such arguments, I'd avoid those "idiots" who had the nerve to think they had created themselves. But I did explore and enjoy other church denominations that had more regimented orders of service (read "shorter"), different doctrinal practices, and diverse social interaction.

Like a lot of people, I made bad choices and experienced hard knocks, setbacks, and struggles during college and in my early twenties. But my "God doesn't care" moment didn't come until after living for years in an unfortunate marriage and then striving to come to terms with my mother's death. To onlookers, it may have seemed that my faith had shattered suddenly, but the truth was that a series of unfortunate events had been eroding my sense of well-being for a long time.

The constant swirl of challenges, including my sister's mental illness, which was hard to recognize when she was young but erupted like a volcano in our living room when she was nineteen, wore me down. And it wasn't just this experience with my sister. Each of my five siblings has dealt with some difficult occurrences, bad breaks, and setbacks that I don't have the right to share here, but as the eldest child, I took these to heart for a lot of reasons.

Now add to the mix my own mistakes, which included unsupportive dating relationships, career frustration, and most of all a crippling battle with low self-esteem and self-doubt. The irony is that people regularly describe me as confident, and my extroverted personality helped hide my struggles. These experiences had been stacking up like a building made from Jenga blocks since my teen years, and when I had to acknowledge that my marriage was a failure and that I'd said "till death do us part" to the wrong man—in front of God and witnesses—the building fell on me, and I was crushed to powder.

I was at the end of my faith. Sprit crushed. Done.

For those of us who believe, faith is the bridge linking his or her spirit to the one believed in—God for me—and when that bridge is no longer stable, a person can become upended by uncontrollable factors.

It's a strange thing how many words we have to name these uncontrollable factors. There are the favorable ones like *serendipity, favor, luck,* and *blessings* that make us feel enchanted. But what about when those uncontrollable factors—like *misfortunes, hassles, foul-ups,* and *curses* make us feel alone and unprotected? How do people of faith deal with those? I found myself drifting amid questions like these in an ocean of uncertainty. Life became like a never-ending scene from Tom Hanks's movie *Cast Away,* except there was no Wilson on my life raft. My prayers felt like futile flares shot into a dark sky. At times I couldn't even grab onto the lifelines people were trying to toss me.

For years upon years, my faith had helped me manage life's uncontrollable factors. It had buoyed me through a severe childhood illness, episodes of extreme bullying, and economic uncertainty. So, when I felt myself drifting, my faith wasn't the only thing I was losing. It was my whole belief system. It was my identity.

As I struggled to wade through these waters, there came another break in the dam: shortly after saying "God doesn't care," I reprised my performance in public—well, almost. During a marriage-counseling session, I virtually smacked the minister's face by spewing out, "I can't trust God." The air shifted during the ensuing second or so of silence. The ministers (a lovely couple who were bonded by decades of solid marital experience) looked pained and stunned. The wife said something like, "You know that's not true; you *know* you can trust God." I wondered how she could be so sure of what *I* knew. My spouse sat sputtering something that I don't even remember.

For me, this was a new, harrowing low point where I hovered for years.

It took all those years after I hit the end of the road with my faith to get up off the mat and decide where faith fit—if at all—in my life. It was no easy prospect to lift myself up, and ultimately I came to the realization that the faith required to get through my forties would have to be vastly different from the faith I'd had in my twenties or at any other point in my life. It took going back to square one—or, in my case, back to my breaking point.

The word *bad* has too many funny, hip, and good connotations to describe my breaking point—also known as the end of my marriage. When my husband told me he would never be able to love me unconditionally, I couldn't blame him. I didn't love myself unconditionally, either. And in my mind, neither did God. It was a full circle of instability and self-doubt.

My tedious and tentative slog back to faith has all of the touchstones of the overcoming-challenges-to-faith stories we enjoy, such as the time when a half-whispered, half-wished prayer was answered the very same week. Or when a friend who had never heard me sing pulled me into his church gospel group, which made me connect in ways I'd neglected for years. My recovery is still in progress, and I don't know what's on the final page. We rarely do, I guess, or it wouldn't be called faith.

I do know that these types of stories tend to have some things in common. There is loss that usually features the death of a loved one, a health challenge, financial ruin, a relationship failure, or a catastrophe. One of these is enough to send a person reeling, but more than one? It's pure faith-crisis fodder.

Let's bring in the emotional responses of anger, distrust, and fear and questions like, "How could you, God?" And then we bargain. This includes promises to get back to our faith, to trust, and to do whatever else seems necessary to *make. It. STOP.* I know. I've been there, promising whatever it takes—whether surrendering any desire or taking on any assignment. Most of us—if not all of us—have.

For me, there were two choices: admitting defeat or resolving my issues. Defeat would mean accepting the miserable drifting, relinquishing faith, and letting life seep out of me. Resolution would mean acceptance, forgiveness, and adjustment. It would mean accepting myself and my path, forgiving offenses, forgiving myself, and forgiving God. (Watch out for the lightning strike!) This process usually begins when the person challenged, the sufferer, is able to embrace the fact that he or she is in a relationship with an unseen person.

And there's the key word: *relationship.*

At some indefinable point, it dawned on me that my "problem" was religion, which was ironically ruining the relationship that helped me build faith. The intricate religious requirements had become my focus, which only made me feel worse. Those requirements didn't soothe doubts and pains. They made people feel unlovable and insufficient if they didn't do things "just right." But when I could see through the haze of my failures and losses, I was able to notice the many coincidences that had pieced together to pull me out of the crisis. A friend would say just the right encouraging words. A situation would resolve in the nick of time. I'd hear a sermon that struck a chord by affirming something I'd believed about God before the great life storms came. When pieced together, they showed a relationship. More importantly, they showed a healthy relationship that wasn't based on perfection. Like all good relationships, it was based on acceptance; it was based on love.

Thank God.

⊰┼⊱

Jennifer Porter is a wordmonger, political junkie, and chocoholic whose favorite question has always been…"Why?"

ASK THE AUTHORS
WHAT WORDS OF ADVICE DO YOU HAVE FOR WOMEN IN THEIR FORTIES?

Shannon Hembree
Be you. Laugh a lot. Rinse. Repeat.

Jen McGinnis
Don't let other people dictate how you feel and what you can and should do. You only need your own approval to decide if you want a family or don't, if you like your job or need a change, if you think you should stay at home or work outside the home. There are a million opinions on what is "appropriate," but you should focus on being true and honest to that gorgeous girl in the mirror. You know what is right. You've made it this far. Trust yourself!

Bree Luck
Stand tall, be a woman, and own these decades!

Sarah Weitzenkorn
Enjoy it. Life is so short. I saw a quote once about how life is like a roller coaster and how you can either scream when there is a bump

or you can throw your hands up and enjoy the ride. Your forties are about enjoying the ride.

Dionne Williams
My advice is this: keep living. I'm sure many women have a bucket list or a vision board. Do everything on the board as much as you can. Set the goals and get them done. Many people out there will be on your team wanting you to finish and pushing you. There will also be those who will look for you to fail. They should be the ones who make you work even harder. Believe in yourself, because that person in the mirror is your biggest opponent.

Anne Karrick Scott Deetsch
Love being forty! Waste no time wishing for the past, and look forward to the person you can be. So much awaits that can be wondrous.

Heather Von St. James
Slow down, take a breath, and realize that you can indeed take control of your life. Learn to say no once in a while, and put yourself first for a change. Now is the time to really start caring for yourself and letting go of toxic people and situations that hold you back. Sit back and enjoy life a little more.

Barbara Fleck
Embrace who you are, and don't compare yourself to others. Remember: that is not your circus; they are not your monkeys.

Elizabeth Pendleton
People are starring in their own show. They are way too busy with their unfolding lives to waste time scrutinizing yours. Be the star of yours, screw the random comment or perceived judgment, and do what you want to do.

Emily Cooke
Don't sweat the small stuff. Life is hard; no need to make it harder for yourself by worrying about things that won't matter in the end. Enjoy who you are now and that you have reached "maturity." Keep friends close, and love with abandon.

Bernadette Jasmine
Love yourself first and foremost, and then you can be a better person for the other people you hold dear in your life. Do something out of your comfort zone. We are only here for a little while, after all. Make time for just you, quiet time to meditate, pray, or reflect—whatever rings true for you—but make time for it even if it means waking up at four in the morning to do so. Quieting your mind is essential to living a relatively stress-free life. Trust me, I know. I am a forty-six-year-old woman, and some days it's the one thing that keeps me sane. Well...that and wine and chocolate.

Vanessa Velez
Embrace it and enjoy it! Age is just a number, so don't let it define your life. Yes, you are in your forties—so what? Don't let that stop you from traveling, dancing, laughing out loud, singing out loud, and embracing your inner twenty-one-year-old every once in a while. I don't think you have to look too hard to find her.

Laura K. Bedingfield
Stop comparing yourself to how you were in your twenties. One day, you'll be in your sixties comparing yourself to how you were in your forties. You can't waste your days longing for the past.

Beckie Cassidy
Don't fear it—embrace it. Yes, your twenties and thirties are gone, but so are the anxieties about how your life will turn out. Your life is just unfolding at forty—and it's quite exciting!

Sarah Freeman Knight

I would tell women to stop worrying so much and to have more fun. I also tell this to myself a hundred times a day.

Jennifer Porter

Embrace life. It sounds so trite, but the present is all you've got. And don't think about age—think about what you desire, and dump anything or anyone who makes you miserable.

Rosanne Nelson

Jump in and don't look back, that's what I say. Try something new, be bold, find your inner voice—and listen to it! Don't allow the noise of others to impact the perception you have of yourself. Don't ask—just do.

Brooke Schmidt

Take it day by day, and stop long enough to enjoy a part of each day.

CHAPTER 17

ON CONFIDENCE:
DON'T ASK, JUST DO

By Rosanne Nelson

Something had to give. I knew that much. The stress had been brewing for quite some time. I was overtaxed at the office, underfocused at home—and swimming in mental chaos.

I was in a new role in a new industry. I was finally reaping the benefits of the hard work accomplished in my twenties and thirties.

The morning started off shakily but oddly predictably. Toddler tears, spilled milk in the unfortunately deep crevices of the car, and a mysteriously missing shoe.

I arrived at the office that day with scattered emotions and frayed nerves. As I typically do when under stress, I immediately took pen to paper. I listed every square inch of work I was responsible for within my role. I was not quite sure what I was going to do with the list at the time, but it was a mental requirement for my sanity. I then listed all family-related items that either needed to be addressed or would soon be around the bend.

The list was voluminous and unwieldy. In terms of work, the responsibilities grew beyond expectation. It was slow and steady, and then one day...it was all-consuming and (somehow) all on me. Visually, I felt like the blow-up clown you see next to the used car lot on a busy road—waving with the wind and balancing spinning plates overhead. Each of my plates was twirling in rapid motion, each extremely fragile, and each carrying the weight of the world. I was talented. I was effective. I was fun to be around. I was drowning.

I didn't realize it then, but I was proving myself at every turn. I was showing up early and staying late. I was the class parent at school and the doting wife at the holiday party. I was the master of spinning plates and lengthy lists.

In my twenties, I'd been focused on showing up and following orders—almost like I was the fortunate one to be shifting papers for others. In my midthirties, I started to gain my voice. It was a slow and low voice, but it was a voice nonetheless. Once I entered my late thirties and children came along, I realized something quite incredible. I owned those plates. Every single one of them. But I knew I'd better gain control. Quickly.

It was a rainy afternoon commute. Thus, what should have taken an hour in Washington, DC, traffic took far more time. I was racing to get the kids from day care. One minute after 6:00 p.m. and we would get charged a late fee and judged for a lifetime. I thought I could make it. I thought time would stand still for me. It did not. I arrived fifteen minutes late to find two very tired kids and a few very frustrated staffers. I could not blame them. By the time we got home, it was 7:00 p.m. You can imagine how that evening went. It wasn't pretty.

I knew I could not live this way any longer. *We* could not live this way any longer. I had a choice, a voice, and self-confidence that had waited years to be unleashed in full force. The time was at hand to start using them.

When I was a young child, my mother would tell me: "Always study in school, because one day, you will want to have options in life and not feel beholden to anyone or anything." She encouraged me to be a nurse so I would have employment options and the ability to jump around in the clinical world. I chose a different path, but I never lost sight of those words: "Never be beholden to anyone or anything."

On that rainy, crummy, chilly night, I reminded myself that I was not beholden to anyone for the decisions I made about my life, my time, my work output, or my effort. In fact, it was quite a powerful moment. The plates stopped spinning. My mind enjoyed long-awaited clarity. I made a decision then and there—a decision about my self-confidence.

What if I lived in a world in which I felt as confident as others looked to be? What if I owned my confidence in such a way that I could control the outcome of a given day? What if I stopped caring about what others thought and relied on my confidence to propel me forward? What if I believed in myself in such a way that I never questioned my value again? What if I served as my own advocate and never questioned it? What if "confidence" was no longer a question but a personal mandate?

Whether it was a firm belief or a simple leap of faith, I didn't have an option. The next morning, I sat down with a cup of coffee, a clear mind, and the list I'd made the day prior. I highlighted the areas within which I would dedicate my time and the areas that would need to be reallocated to others. I considered the impact this might have on how my senior leadership might perceive me. I considered the notion that I could be reprimanded for asserting such bold direction on my behalf. I considered what the "worst case" could look like. And then I set up a meeting with my executive vice president.

Confidence, especially with women, is a funny thing. I believe we find our confidence rhythm in our forties, because we spend our twenties and thirties finding our way in and around minefields. By the time I hit forty, I simply stopped caring what others thought. It wasn't that I didn't care about those closest to me—of course I did. But I put my own self-confidence above all else. It was liberating.

People took notice and eventually asked me what I was doing differently. It's not magic, but it does take effort.

I didn't *ask* if I could meet with my EVP to address workload. *I* set it up. When I arrived at her office, I didn't *ask* if we could sit together on the couch; I simply sat on the couch and leveraged my body language to assert control of the meeting. I didn't ask for her guidance on shifting work around; I simply apprised her of the direction I was going to go and told her how I planned to accomplish the effort. I stopped asking if it was okay to leave early for an appointment. I stopped apologizing for childcare issues that were part of my day-to-day existence. I stopped putting value in others' unknown and unexpressed thoughts of me and my decisions.

After that moment, guess what happened. Nothing. And everything.

I recognized so clearly that everyone has baggage, and we all have a choice on how to pack it. I also realized that I'm the only person on this planet who can control my choices and my direction. Confidence is not about running for president, but it *is* about running your life. It's about leading yourself authentically, with humility...and with a lot of baggage.

You see, in my twenties—and even up to my midthirties—I would have kept going at my breakneck pace. I would have accepted it as normal. I would have made excuses and apologized for early departures and late arrivals. I would have projected my emotions in such a way that allowed others to control my response or workload. I would have said yes far more times than I would have said no. I would have been true to everyone else but me.

Our little ones are no longer in diapers, but they still need to be picked up and dropped off within a specific time frame. Our minivan is still covered with cheerios, and that spilled milk has long since dried up. But now there's a confidence to my day. At forty-one, I don't ask. I just do. At forty-one, I am not beholden to anyone other than my loving family. At forty-one, I have a voice that is both powerful and purposeful. At forty-one, I have confidence.

As I look back on my twenties and thirties, I don't always recognize the person reflected back. In fact, I remember coming home from my first job after college and crying, "Is this it? This *can't* be it." On some level, that served as a critical turning point for me. I learned how to fake confidence, or at least present myself as someone who knew far more than I did at the time. I think to some degree we all find ourselves pretending during those years. Pretending to know the answers, pretending to know the path ahead, pretending to know ourselves. I was that classic photo of a young girl wearing her mother's heels. I was cute, but I was pretending.

Even still, I am proud of that version of me. I believe that version needed to exist in order for me to grow into who I am today… as a wife, a mother, a friend, a fortysomething. Confidence was not an overnight transformation for me. It took more times falling down than I'd like to admit, but those years also forced me to get back up…and grow into the person I am today—a confident fortysomething who is not beholden to anything—but immensely grateful for everything.

So, go ahead and make your list. Decide what's important to you, and resolve to make it happen. Don't ask, just do.

⟞⧾⧾⟝

Rosanne Nelson is a leadership-development consultant by day and a mother of two confident little girls by night. She enjoys telling her husband about the twentysomething version of herself and remains grateful the Internet was not around during those years.

CHAPTER 18

ON THE LOSS OF A PARENT:
HOW I GRIEVED, COPED, AND LEARNED TO LIVE DIFFERENTLY AFTER MY FATHER DIED

By Brooke Schmidt

I stirred instant pasta. Poured a glass of water. I actually lived for a couple of hours not knowing yet that he was dead. I just stood in my kitchen while my nearly two-year-old napped—finally, peacefully, blessedly. Me, pouring processed seasonings into boiling water for a quick, late lunch—thankful for something other than a toddler's leftover hot-dog pieces—having no idea he had died. Shouldn't the earth have moved beneath me? Shouldn't I have felt it in my body—a shudder, a chill, a skipped heartbeat? Shouldn't I have known the loss without having to be told?

Apparently not.

I stood in the kitchen, wiping crumbs from the counter and giving my husband a wondering smile as he burst through the back door hours before he was due home. I asked him what he was doing home, but I knew before I had finished speaking. Only then, standing over the stove, staring at the man interrupting my sacred "the child is napping" stretch, did I know my father was gone.

"Why didn't you tell me?" I yelled. Funny, because he *was* telling me.

Even then, I recognized the wrongness of having lived those minutes not knowing my father had died, the time it had taken my mother to call my husband with instructions to make sure he was with me when I heard the news. The time it had taken my husband to make arrangements at work, to pack up his laptop, to accept condolences from engineers, the men pounding his shoulder, saying, "Sorry, man" as he made his way hastily to the office parking lot. The time it had taken him to drive across the city. I changed a diaper, read a book—probably *Bear Snores On*, which to this day I can recite because I read it countless times during my son's "again" phase—sang a lullaby, stirred artificially flavored chicken noodles, lived without knowing my world was changed. Even now, almost eight years later, it's maddening, irritating, unbelievable that the world actually continues to turn when someone dies. How ridiculously cliché.

The truth is that everything had changed months before. The winter prior, Dad had started having trouble swallowing. I was thirty and living in another state, trying to keep my head above water, swimming in the duties of mothering a "spirited" toddler, managing life with a traveling husband, and staring at the glow of a computer late at night, keeping up with freelance writing projects. I gave my father's swallowing issue little thought. He was my father, after all. My father, who had provided an idyllic childhood for my twin brother and me. My father, who managed companies without a formal college education. My father, who made rooms of people roll with laughter every time he spoke. My father, for whom I had never worried. For whom I had never realized I *should* worry. My mother had hardly seemed concerned as she mentioned it over the phone. I was busy figuring out how to keep my child from having a tantrum every time he needed to wear socks. You remember those days of toddlerhood, trying to have a phone conversation:

"Okay, Mom. Let me know what the doctor says. Hold on. Don't! Eat! That! Put that...no! Mom, I've gotta go."

It's odd, even now, to look back and take in how naive I was. Sure, I was a grown-up. A college grad, married nine years, a parent myself. My uncle, my mom's brother, had died from a heart attack when I was four and he just thirty-six with an infant and wife at home. But I was too little to understand the magnitude of that tragedy, the complete injustice of a child growing up with no memory of his father at all. Each of my grandparents had passed away years before—two I'd barely known, and two I had adored. I spent several summers at my grandpa's side in his golden recliner, reading books, snuggled into his warmth, while my grandma doted on us both. His sudden death in my thirteenth year was so, so sad, but I viewed it simply as what happens. Grandparents are old, and they die. How wonderfully childlike of me. My mother's mother lived to see my wedding day; she was a woman so exceptional that my daughter bears her middle name. When she died, I was in my twenties; I saw her passing as a huge loss yet still a part of the natural circle of life. I recognized the blessing of being all grown up and still having had a grandparent in my life.

In my early thirties, it hadn't yet occurred to me that my heart could be shattered. I know that sounds terribly lucky. I just wasn't the girl to whom bad things happened. I wore my seat belt; I said no to drugs; I guarded my heart. In my teenage years, as I read Judy Blume and Jane Austen, and later in my writing classes, I lamented that I had no sad stories. In college, one of my roommate's mothers died after a long illness. The experience was wrenching. And still, I remained secure, even oblivious, to the idea that death would ever come for my own parents. I suppose that's part of the gift my father gave me—a childhood so full of love, a sense of self so bold, an overarching love so strong, that I believed us indestructible. He was too reliable to not be relied upon. He was forever there. A reality in which my father was not alive simply didn't exist, and as I plowed forward with my own life, I never stopped to consider that which was impossible.

Over the last several years, the details have gotten hazy, the timeline blurry, of how our family learned that a prescription from a local doctor wasn't going to fix my dad's swallowing issue. At first, he was flat out told not to worry. "It's not cancer," they told my parents. And yet no one could solve the problem, fix my father so that he could participate in the most basic human need and pleasure: eating. Oh, how our family could eat. Dad was known around his neighborhood as the man who could fire up a grill and produce the perfect filet mignon or London broil. And he cooked the ultimate slice of crispy bacon. My father was both the ice-cream scooper and the popcorn popper when our childhood evenings were filled with treats. In my younger years, I kept my seat at the family dinner table until I finished my milk—and my meat and potatoes. Not that our meals were all *Leave It to Beaver* all the time: There was that evening my brother threw a basket of piping-hot dinner rolls in Dad's face. My brother finished his supper in his room.

So, when Dad continued to find it impossible to swallow, as the pounds slipped away, as everything he chewed got stuck in his chest, my parents headed to the experts at the Mayo Clinic in Jacksonville, Florida. Here, where the country's best doctors were, surely he would be offered a solution. They believed the little flap between Dad's esophagus and stomach was in spasm. The idea was to do a simple procedure in which the flap was injected with Botox to stop it from contracting on its own. I believed we would soon hear from the doctors: "Ta-da! Sir, we've paralyzed your esophageal sphincter; please enjoy a steak again."

I left our one-year-old son with my husband in Georgia and road tripped down to Jacksonville to be with Mom while Operation Botox occurred. We sat in waiting rooms, heard strangers' sometimes gloomy, sometimes poignant tales of illness, and joked about needing our own Botox injections. We waited too long. What was supposed to be a simple enough procedure clearly wasn't, although neither Mom nor I mentioned the passing time to one another.

I don't have a clear picture in my mind of how we were told or who did the telling—that they couldn't do the Botox injection. The tool they placed down Dad's esophagus couldn't get to the flap; it bumped into something. Something they went ahead and biopsied. Something that was a tumor. I still think of it as some kind of darkly magic tumor. Ladies and gentlemen, step right up to see the one, the only, the completely imperceptible tumor that fooled even the famous Mayo Clinic doctors in test after test after test.

Esophageal cancer is what it is called. A cancer that comes with a fairly dismal survival statistic. A cancer that receives almost no research funding but is the fastest-growing cancer diagnosis in the United States. A cancer linked to long-term acid reflux, a condition my father suffered from for as long as I can remember, and a condition that no doctor ever mentioned could cause cancer. As all those years passed, as Dad received pill after pill for heartburn symptoms, no one ever said, "You should get an annual endoscopy to screen for cancer." And, really, even if Dad had been told that, his tumor had seemed invisible to even the best doctors with the most state-of-the-art tests for all those months.

Other than waving long-term acid reflux around as a red flag, esophageal cancer is a mostly silent killer. The main symptom of esophageal cancer is trouble swallowing. And by the time you have trouble swallowing, you're probably in big trouble. Dad was. One day after his diagnosis, he was surgically implanted with a feeding tube and a chemotherapy port. A bold, hilarious, and—up until now—relatively healthy fifty-seven-year-old man, a father who could do anything and whose infectious smile always convinced you that you could too, was being fed medical liquids straight into his intestines. Maybe I should have seen it as writing on the wall, the stark metaphor of a magnificent man sustained by such a device. But I was stubborn.

Dad and I immediately set up a CarePages.com site to efficiently update friends and family. My type A tendencies and willingness to put almost anything, no matter how personal, in writing are clearly inherited traits. The web page provided a creative outlet and a distraction, and it offered each of us some shred of control in an out-of-control situation. The entries on Dad's CarePages today serve as a harsh reminder of how quickly and painfully we lost him. Just seven months after Operation Botox was a bust, Dad was gone. The adenocarcinoma cells had spread to his bones; all his torturous chemotherapy was basically useless. Typically, if esophageal cancer is going to spread, you'll find it in the liver or some other organ. Spreading to the bones? Almost never. Dad always did stand out. Leave it to him not to do cancer like everyone else.

Five months after Dad's cancer diagnosis, we began the long good-bye. I recognized right away that the opportunity to say good-bye was an offering many families don't receive, even if I wasn't happy about it. When you know someone is dying, when you've been given a specific amount of time, you get very busy saying good-bye. For me, it all seemed a bit like an out-of-body experience; this was happening to some other family, right? I have vivid memories of Dad explaining to my mom, my brother, and me the hymns we should play at his funeral. I recall lecturing him on the utter obnoxiousness of the conversation, of the notebook in which he was making his own funeral notes. I remember storming off to their guest room in disgust. My father does not accept a death sentence. Except that apparently, he does. He recognized when he had a choice and when he didn't.

He had endured five months of debilitating chemotherapy with little to show for it. Mercifully, the tumor in his esophagus had disappeared following painful radiation, allowing the feeding tube to be removed. Before he died, Dad even enjoyed a filet from

Ruth's Chris Steakhouse. It wasn't as good as the ones he'd made over the years, but still. It certainly was better than a can of Boost and a spoonful of Jell-O.

Despite the lesions covering his bones, Dad was determined to use his newfound ability to swallow and to complete tasks such as planning his own funeral and apologizing for all his perceived parenting mistakes. If my father was talking at all over those last eight weeks, it was to tell us all how much he loved us. And how much Jesus loved us. The Jesus talk was really out of character for a man who had a library of off-color jokes in his repertoire. Sure, Dad had survived the nuns in Catholic school, and my parents had taken us to church every Sunday when we were kids. We wore white and had a First Communion and thanked the Lord for our daily bread each night, but the Son of God wasn't part of our typical family conversations until cancer came along. I managed to torment Dad in his last weeks by debating the meaning of life and the existence of a loving God who would allow a fine man such as Dad to be physically tortured. What kind of God would rob me of my father?

"Well, Brooke," Dad would say, carrying his Bible, "if Jesus can endure dying on the cross to save mankind, I can endure this."

Well, okay, Dad. I'm here to tell you a little understanding of that which surpasses understanding would be handy when someone you love is dying much too soon. But Dad kept the faith.

Dad also managed to pass along his legendary turkey-carving skills to both my brother and my husband at his last Thanksgiving and Christmas. I'm not sure even I can find the words to describe what happened to my soul watching my by then slight father stand in our kitchen that last December, just days before his death, patiently showing my dear husband, my twin at his side, how to carve the family's famously buttered holiday turkey.

When my parents left my house that Christmas to go home to Florida, we both knew it would be our last good-bye. He stood at my back door, the car already loaded with baggage and my mother there waiting. He was wearing a cream-colored sweater and holding a stylish wooden cane to help support his aching bones. He held the door open a bit, letting December's chill drift through the kitchen and swirl around our emptied Christmas tree.

I had imagined a lot of moments in my life, perhaps morbidly. In an effort to "have a plan," I had imagined what I would do if my house burned down, if my car crashed, if a tree fell on the roof. I ran through all the steps in my head and located the emergency exits. But I had never known that I should have readied myself to tell my dad good-bye. Tears streamed down his face—only the third time I'd ever really seen him cry—and in that moment, I tried to be brave. Tried to stay on my feet as he told me he was sorry he was dying, he was sorry he had to leave me. "It's okay," we told each other. It was the little white lie we left hanging in the air between us as he walked down the driveway.

My parents made it home to their house in Florida, a place my dad liked to call "paradise." It was there, in their bedroom, under the care of hospice, that Dad rapidly declined in those last few days, unable to have any more conversations. And when he passed away, I didn't know until I was told.

Four months after Dad died, my husband and I found out I was pregnant with our second child. Our little girl entered this world on the first anniversary of my father's death—well before her due date. She's an addition to our world who makes a bitter day sweet. I'm keenly aware that the day would have been much sweeter had my father actually lived to see it, but she is the clearest kind of sign, a tangible reminder, that life must go on. Why must I get out of bed with a shattered heart? Because there are people. People who need me. As much as I expected time to stop when Dad died, time's passing was also the only way through.

Despite my daughter's serendipitous timing, which I am told should bring me immense amounts of peace and a certain belief in Heaven or some kind of afterlife—because, of course, there's no such thing as coincidence—I've wrestled ugly feelings to the ground over the last years. My peace and understanding aren't always peaceful or present.

Guilt has been conspicuous. Brooke, I tell myself, you had a father in your life. A good one. You're supposed to be grateful. You're supposed to be humbled. People have sadder stories than this. Some people don't even know their dads. Your grief isn't justified; there are starving kids in Africa and earthquakes in Haiti and mad men in movie theaters. You had thirty-one years as the daughter of a great man. Get over yourself.

But I can't help but think how absolutely unfair it is that my children will never know the man who raised me to be their mother. If I could, I'd rip photographs off my walls and stamp my feet and scream nonsense. But what kind of example would that be for the kids to whom I'm forever saying, "Use your words" and "Life isn't fair. You don't always get what you want"?

Oh, *how* you don't always get what you want. Tantrums won't make it so. Other people have much better reasons than I do to throw fits.

Mourning the loss of expectations I had for my life, and my children's lives, that I had never even verbalized was a huge part of the grieving process.

I expected my children would nestle into my father's recliner to read books each summer.

I expected my father to take my kids golfing.

I expected my father to know my children.

I expected my father to be.

I simply did not know he could be lost. Along with his loss was the loss of an entire future I hadn't even known I had imagined.

Several times after his death, I picked up my phone to call Dad—to share a story of work or parenting or to ask his advice. Every time I had to set my phone back down on the counter because he wouldn't be on the other end felt like a punch to my gut—as if my heart had ripped open again. How could he not be alive? How could I keep forgetting? How was I still breathing if he didn't exist? The forgetting and remembering again can drive you crazy. How could I have a child of my own and feel so childlike, a lost little girl in her thirties?

All the books about grief are right: you just learn to live differently. You're changed. And soon enough, you don't forget again. No more punch to your gut when you think, My dad is dead.

Today, as I stare down my fortieth year, my father's death is still the greatest heartbreak of my life. I haven't wrapped my mind around the idea that his early death is part of a great plan we'll all someday understand. His death is still not okay—and that's what I've accepted. Some things simply aren't okay. My questions are okay. My grief, even if I feel it eight years later, is okay. It's okay to invite anger in to sit a spell. The key, I've had to learn, is to be bold enough to open the door and kick anger out when its welcome's worn thin. I don't believe my father died a painful death to teach me any life lessons, but I do believe it's up to me to choose what I learn from the loss; it's up to me to choose to continue to be the person my father helped me become. Every day, I get to choose.

I hate what we are missing without my father in our lives. But I don't let our loss consume me. As they say, he wouldn't want that—for my family or for me. The emptiness of his space in this world is something I will always feel, but I have no choice other than to fill it as best I can with the same love and laughter he offered while he was here. That's the legacy I have to honor.

I know today that the conviction I carried throughout the first part of my life—that my parents would simply always exist—contributed in countless ways to the person I was for all those years—and to the person I am now. The methods by which my father instilled in me such a bold security, such a confidence in my roots that I could go and take flight without fear of falling, remain intangible to me. But I hope—I so hope—that I'm giving his beautiful grandchildren that same immovable foundation. I hope they someday know it's because of their grandfather that I will always catch them should they fall.

Brooke Schmidt, freelance editor and writer, lives with her engineer husband, two kids, and two rescue dogs in the 'burbs of Atlanta.

CHAPTER 19

ON FRIENDSHIP:
BONJOUR, DEAR DIARY

By Shannon Hembree

I wondered for a long while whether I could write both the beginning and ending chapters of this book...but then I remembered that I was the one pulling together all of the chapters and decided I could do whatever I want. (Stay tuned for the chapter on power grabs by slightly crazy writers!) So, here we go.

Friendship, like anything else, takes work—not all the time, but it does take an investment of ourselves. There's less effort when we're younger...unless you count suppressing your little-girl outrage when your friend loses your Strawberry Shortcake necklace or tells you she can put beautiful braids in your My Little Pony's tail and winds up getting it forever stuck in a tangle. Okay, maybe there's a lot of effort when you're little, but it's a different effort. An *easier* effort—at least when you compare it to your adult friendships. Those days of My Little Pony angst are so long gone now that I can't even remember them in a clear timeline of images.

The friendships I had in my teens are more vivid, and thankfully many of those friendships are still holding strong today.

These friendships were—like everything else in my teenage life—intense. Part of this was driven by teenage life in general, and part of it was driven by the fact that I went to an all-girls boarding school. I mean, how can you *not* have intense friendships when you're having naked pillow fights all the time? I'm totally kidding, but you'd be surprised how many people (only men, actually) ask if we did that.

These were the girls I literally grew up with. Journey back with me mentally to a time before cell phones. It's hard not to form lifelong bonds when there's no TV in your room, cell phones don't exist, and your campus is located in the middle of nowhere. Quite simply, it was perfect. Okay, not perfect. There were mean girls there, too, who thought they were all that and a bag of FUNYUNS (blech!), but all in all, it was great.

We spent hours on end going for walks and staying up late talking about everything. How many hours did I spend with one amazing friend in particular, dissecting the many ways in which I was sabotaging my relationship with the first love of my life and how my dad's terrible choices were dooming me to my own disastrous relationships? Because that is what friends are—the sounding boards for our madness, the counterpoints to our self-doubt, and the companions as we grow into ourselves. I don't always talk to these friends from high school. I certainly don't talk to them often, but when I do, it's like being transported back to another place entirely.

And Lordy, old friends are some of the best kinds of friends to have around. They remember you with your hair parted down the middle and feathered on the sides. (How I never actually took flight in a strong breeze, I'll never know!) They are the friends who, if you read your teen-angst diary aloud, would laugh and smile and say, "I totally remember that."

I actually went through my high school diary at one point and found a number of entries I would use if I went to one of those diary-poetry slams where you read your own entries up on stage (which will never happen given that I have a crippling fear of public speaking). One of these entries starts, "Bonjour, Dear Diary..." Because, you know...I'm French and all. Side note, this was also around the time I saw *Les Misérables* and started signing my diary entries "Cossette," which is a true testament to my high school friends, because who the hell could put up with that? It's also a true testament to my friends now, because I am still that same sort of chronically obsessed-with-something person who is easily distracted by anything and everything...look, a squirrel! And in that vein of being easily taken off track, here are a few little gems from my high school diary that I will totally connect back to friendship once I figure out how to do that...

Bonjour, Dear Diary...
In school I'm reading Robinson Crusoe, *and it's pointless. It's boring and stupid and nothing happens. I'm going to go watch* Days of Our Lives.

Bonjour, Dear Diary...
I know what his cologne smells like, and once at school someone must have had it on, because after I touched this door, my hand smelled like it. I went around all day, smelling my hand. I know I must like him even though I would never admit it.

Bonjour, Dear Diary...
It was so cute. He showed me how to find the North Star from the Little Dipper, and he named the tiniest dipper we saw "Shannon's Dipper." I think I love him.

Pretty awesome, right? And I think the friend connection I was looking for there is that my friends—old and new—know that I am an easily distracted big old dork, and they love me anyway. Because isn't that friendship? Loving your friends, warts and all? This is especially true now that we are all grown up and there just isn't time to sit around for ten hours over coffee dissecting every detail of every word uttered after going out the night before.

More often than not, unless my girlfriends and I make a point to go out alone, our conversations are interrupted by little ones sneaking into the cabinet and eating a whole box of cookies (really happened) or little hands reaching into the toilet to fish out a toy (also true). Long-lasting, in-depth communication is just not possible when your kids are young unless you park them in front of the TV for the duration, which as we all know is tantamount in today's society to dipping them in toxic sludge.

Despite these time constraints and very real challenges to our sanity, our friendships do survive as we get older, and the older we get and the more we live, the more complex the challenges become and the more important our friends become. The shit has gotten more real, so to speak. Mortality is no longer a far-off thing that will never happen to us; it is something we recognize could actually happen. And it's not just something that *could* happen; it is something to plan for. Who will get custody of the kids if we both die? Do we have enough life insurance? My friends and I used to exercise with the goal of going out and finding Mr. Right. Now we exercise to keep our hearts healthy and to keep disease at bay. Even the workouts are different. They focus more on how to address problem areas after having children than they do on having the hottest abs on the beach. Such is life.

Friendship now—like always, really—is a back-and-forth exercise of picking your friends up when they are down and having them do the same for you. The only thing is that as you get older, the picking up can be harder to do. How do you pick up a friend when the love of her life has died? Or when she has been desperately trying to get pregnant, does, and then has a miscarriage? Or her husband leaves her? Or she has been told she has cancer? Or she has found out that her child has an incurable disease? The older we get, the more these things come to pass. All of them have happened to friends of mine. These are the times when it can be the hardest to be a friend—not because we don't want to, but because holy hell, how do you do it? You can't change the situation or make it better. You can't bring back what was lost or turn the tide on an unwanted fate. You can, however, be there. And being there is one of the most important parts of the whole friend thing—whether it's in person or in spirit. Both matter.

My friends have come through with flying colors for me in many wretched spots. I have had friends come to my house to watch two of my kids while I have taken my other child to the emergency room for an asthma attack or whatever medical emergency they had that day—you can insert a lot here, from broken bones to bleeding gashes. Bottles of wine have shown up on my doorstep during particularly tough weeks (my friends know me well), as have doughnuts and cupcakes (ditto). We have all been through our struggles, and somewhere in those struggles, we have found each other and supported each other, because that is what friends do—whether they are new friends or old friends and whether it is something as heart-wrenching as a funeral for someone who died far, far too young or something as insane as parasailing for the first time with a friend who shares your fear of heights (and fear of being eaten by a shark, because parasailing over the ocean for people like this is *super* smart).

That sense of being there for each other is evident throughout these chapters—chapters written by different women from different backgrounds and experiences. It is one of the universal threads that keep us sane. And yes, it's something that is there for the hardest of times, but it is also there in the most mundane of times. One of my favorite things to do is going out with friends and having a good laugh. I'm not talking a little chuckle. I'm talking a full-on, hysterical bout of laughter that you can't stop—where the tears come to your eyes and you think afterward that you miss laughing like that and need to do it more often. Because between making the school lunches and driving from gymnastics to basketball to violin, it isn't always so easy to get together with friends and let yourself go and just laugh. I miss laughing like that. And I miss spending an hour on the phone gabbing with friends about what is going on in my life and theirs. I miss hanging out with my friends for no reason at all.

And that may wind up being the biggest blessing of being forty thus far. As we get older, our kids get older. Phone conversations with friends are getting longer. I'm making a point to go out more with friends, because I know I don't have to be up every two hours (or every thirty minutes in the case of twins) with a newborn. I'm slowly but surely carving out more time for me, and my friends are starting to do the same. It's a freeing and healthy thing. You might even say it's a forties thing.

Friendship in my forties includes new friends, like gymnastics moms (gasp) who aren't as crazy as you might have heard (not all of them, anyway) and who have become bright lights in my life over the last couple of years. They have brought levity to my life during difficult times—like when my daughter broke her ankle during a gymnastics practice—and they have kept me sane by taking, but not posting on Facebook, embarrassing photos of us when we have gone out for various celebrations.

My forties friendships also include old friends—friends from high school, whom I grew up with in so many ways—and friends I met during college, graduate school, and beyond. These friends have somehow become a part of my being. They are the ones who did my makeup at my wedding and who held up my wedding dress while I peed. (Doesn't everyone have that friend?) They have shared my clothes (and in one case, a toothbrush on vacation, unless that crosses a line for what we are supposed to share here); they have worried with me over my kids' illnesses and various medical issues; and they have commiserated with me on our irresponsible youth in the sun that landed me with a skin-cancer diagnosis. They are the godmothers to my kids, the voice of reason when I am not being reasonable, and the soul sisters to my being. After all those years of friendship together and after all our shared experiences, it's safe to say that a part of them has been forever woven into me.

It is both of these types of friends—old and new—who help you write your stories of friendship that no one else on this earth can tell. They share the memories you can laugh at together that no one else gets—the stories they could no doubt blackmail you with forever and ever. It is these friends who get you through the highs and lows of life and who are slowly but surely climbing out of their parenting shells with you to once again chat or hang out on a regular basis. Because in our forties, as we reach the point when we are introducing our not-so-young-anymore kids to books like *The Care and Keeping of You*, we are also remembering the importance of the care and keeping of ourselves. That care and keeping involves not only taking the time for our own well-being but also taking the time for our friends, because they are a part of the fabric of our well-being, too. In fact, they are a core part of it.

So, here is my challenge to you after reading this collection of amazing stories written by amazing women. Take a moment over the next couple of days to plan something with a friend. Plan to get coffee. Plan to get dinner. Plan a walk or a talk or something in between, but plan *something.* For you. For them. For the friendships that remind us of who we used to be (winged hair and all), of how strong we truly are (aside from my inability to resist frosted cupcakes), and of how many exciting adventures we have yet to embark on (girls' weekend in NYC!). Maybe even start a journal with a friend bucket list of things you want to do and girls' weekends you want to take over the next couple of years and beyond.

How great would it be to look over that list in another forty years and say that you accomplished all those things and to laugh at all the hilarious details of how they played out? (Because we all know there would be hilarious details.) As a matter of fact, I'm starting my very own journal bucket list right now. I don't know what will be on it, but I do know the perfect way to start it, and it goes a little something like this: *Bonjour, Dear Diary...*

Shannon Hembree is continually amazed by the strength, compassion, and power of women the world over and is looking forward to many more decades of watching this crazy thing called life unfold.

No matter the decade you claim as your own, we wish you joy, peace, friendship, and love in whatever way works for you.

Cheers!

Shannon, Jen M., Bree, Sarah W., Dionne, Anne Karrick, Heather, Barbara, Elizabeth, Emily, Bernadette, Vanessa, Laura, Beckie, Sarah K., Jennifer P., Rosanne, and Brooke

Made in the USA
Columbia, SC
11 September 2019